INTRODUCTION TO THE WORLD'S MAJOR RELIGIONS

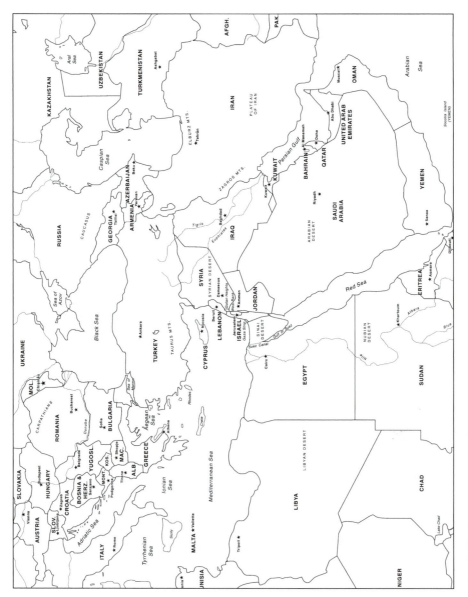

The Middle East. Cartography by Mapcraft.

Introduction to the World's Major Religions

JUDAISM

Volume 1

Emily Taitz

Lee W. Bailey, General Editor

GREENWOOD PRESS
Westport, Connecticut • London

Library of Congress Cataloging-in-Publication Data
available on request from the Library of Congress.

British Library Cataloguing in Publication Data is available.

Copyright © 2006 by Emily Taitz

All rights reserved. No portion of this book may be
reproduced, by any process or technique, without the
express written consent of the publisher.

ISBN 0–313–33634–2 (set)
    0–313–33327–0 (vol. 1)
    0–313–32724–6 (vol. 2)
    0–313–33251–7 (vol. 3)
    0–313–32683–5 (vol. 4)
    0–313–32846–3 (vol. 5)
    0–313–33590–7 (vol. 6)

First published in 2006

Greenwood Press, 88 Post Road West, Westport, CT 06881
An imprint of Greenwood Publishing Group, Inc.
www.greenwood.com

Printed in the United States of America

The paper used in this book complies with the
Permanent Paper Standard issued by the National
Information Standards Organization (Z39.48–1984).

10 9 8 7 6 5 4 3 2 1

Introduction to the World's Major Religions
Lee W. Bailey, General Editor

*To Isaac, whose enthusiasm for this project
encouraged me every step of the way*

CONTENTS

SET FOREWORD

This set, *Introduction to the World's Major Religions,* was developed to fill a niche between sophisticated texts for adults and the less in-depth references for middle schoolers. It includes six volumes on religions from both Eastern and Western traditions: Judaism, Christianity, Islam, Hinduism, Confucianism and Taoism, and Buddhism. Each volume gives a balanced, accessible introduction to the religion.

Each volume follows a set format so readers can easily find parallel information in each religion. After a Timeline and Introduction, narrative chapters are as follows: the "History of Foundation" chapter describes the founding people, the major events, and the most important decisions made in the faith's early history. The "Texts and Major Tenets" chapter explains the central canon, or sacred texts, and the core beliefs, doctrines, or tenets, such as the nature of deities, the meaning of life, and the theories of the afterlife. The chapter on "Branches" outlines the major divisions of the religion, their reasons for being, their distinctive doctrines, their historical background, and structures today. The chapter on "Practice Worldwide" describes the weekly worship practices, the demographic statistics indicating the sizes of various branches of religions, the global locations, and historical turning points. The chapter on "Rituals and Holidays" describes the ritual practices of the religions in all their varieties and the holidays worldwide, such as the Birth of the Buddha, as they have developed historically. The chapter on "Major Figures" covers selected notable people in the history of each religion and their important influence. A glossary provides definitions for major special terms, and the index gives an alphabetic locator for major themes. A set index is included in volume 6 (to facilitate comparison).

In a world of about 6 billion people, today the religion with the greatest number of adherents is Christianity, with about 2 billion members, comprising 33 percent of the globe's population. Next largest is Islam, with about 1.3 billion members, (about 22 percent). Hindus number about 900 million (about 15 percent). Those who follow traditional Chinese religions number about 225 million (4 percent). Although China has the world's largest population, it is officially Communist, and Buddhism has been blended with traditional Confucianism and Taoism, so numbers in China are difficult to verify. Buddhism claims about 360 million members (about 6 percent of the world's population). Judaism, although historically influential, has a small number of adherents—about 14 million (0.2 percent of the world's population). These numbers are constantly shifting, because religions are always changing and various surveys define groups differently.[1]

Religions are important elements of the worldview of a culture. They express, for example, the cultural beliefs about cosmology, or picture of the universe (e.g., created by God or spontaneous), and the origin of humanity (e.g., purposeful or random), its social norms (e.g., monogamy or polygamy), its ways of relating to ultimate reality (e.g., sacrifice or obedience to law), the historical destiny (e.g., linear or cyclical), life after death (e.g., none or judgment), and ethics (e.g., tribal or universal).

As the world gets smaller with modern communications and global travel, people come in contact with those of other religions far more frequently than in the past. This can cause conflicts or lead to cooperation, but the potential for hostile misunderstanding is so great that it is important to foster knowledge and understanding. Noting parallels in world religions can help readers understand each religion better. Religions can provide ethical guidance that can help solve serious cultural problems. During war the political question "why do they hate us?" may have serious religious aspects in the answer. New answers to the question of how science and religion in one culture can be reconciled may come from another religion's approach. Scientists are increasingly analyzing the ecological crisis, but the solutions will require more than new technologies. They will also require ethical restraint, the motivation to change the destructive ecological habits of industrial societies, and some radical revisioning of worldviews. Other contemporary issues, such as women's rights, will also require patriarchal religions to undertake self-examination. Personal faith is regularly called into consideration with daily news of human destructiveness or in times of crisis, when the very meaning of life comes into question. Is life basically good? Will goodness in the big picture overcome immediate evil? Should horrendous behavior be forgiven? Are people alone in a huge, indifferent universe, or is the ultimate reality a caring, just power behind the scenes of human and cosmic history? Religions offer various approaches, ethics, and motivations to deal with such issues. Readers can use the books in this set to rethink their own beliefs and practices.

NOTE

1. United Nations, "Worldwide Adherents of All Religions by Six Continental Areas, Mid-2002," *World Population Prospects: The 1998 Revision* (New York: United Nations, 1999).

ACKNOWLEDGMENTS

I would like to thank, first and foremost, Rabbi Myron Fenster, who took the time to read this manuscript and share with me his many areas of expertise. This book would not be complete without his help. Also, I thank my dear friend and colleague, Sondra Henry, who critiqued what I wrote and constantly challenged me to make it clearer and better.

Adele Lobel, a photo researcher at the Jewish Theological Seminary, helped me obtain some of the photos in this volume, and Rona Lupkin, librarian at Temple Israel of Great Neck, New York, generously gave me free run of the library. Many thanks to both of them.

Thanks are due as well to Carol and Arthur Anderman, Norma Grill, Leonard Karpel and Willa Morris. These knowledgeable friends were always available when I needed a sounding board for my ideas, and they graciously shared their own valuable opinions with me.

Harold Fink, my computer guru, gave me constant technical support, for which I am always grateful.

A special thanks to the late Rabbi Mordecai Waxman, whose teaching and inspiration over thirty years found its way into my head and into my heart.

Finally, I want to thank my husband, Isaac, for his support and advice, and for all the times he made lunch for me when I was immersed in research for this book.

INTRODUCTION

Judaism is counted among the world's great religions and is often credited with being the originator of monotheism, the belief in a single and
unique God. Monotheism, as well as the core group of basic tenets, laws,
and practices first laid out in the Hebrew Bible, established the foundations
for many other religions, especially Christianity and Islam. But Judaism
contains several other components in addition to religious faith, making it
more complicated to define.

First, there is a national component. Many people believe that, in addition to a religion, being Jewish is a nationality, an allegiance to the same
nation state. In ancient times Jews did originally belong to one nation, a
small country located in western Asia on the Mediterranean Sea. During
the early ninth century before the Common Era (B.C.E.), that nation divided
into two separate kingdoms: Israel in the north and Judah in the south.
Then the Assyrians conquered Israel, the Northern Kingdom, in 722 B.C.E.
The Israelites were sent into exile and their land disappeared from the map
of the Middle East. Only Judah, the tiny nation centered around Jerusalem, remained for several more centuries until Rome finally destroyed it in
68–70 C.E. and forced most of the Jews to leave.

From 70 C.E., even though some Jews always lived in that area, there was
no Jewish nation until the modern state of Israel was reestablished in 1948.
Through all those centuries, traditional Jews remained a separate people
and clung to the idea that one day the Messiah would come and lead them
back to their land. The majority of Jews living in the twenty-first century no

longer believe in a Messiah, but most are concerned about Israel and have some allegiance to its existence as a Jewish State. Yet most Jews are loyal citizens of other nations and do not plan to move to Israel.

If Jews were originally a single nation, is Judaism, then, also an ethnic group? Many people, including some Jews, believe this. But if an ethnic group is a group that claims a common origin, similar physical characteristics, and a shared history, this certainly does not define Judaism today. Jews encompass every racial group. They may resemble the darkest Africans or the lightest skinned northern Europeans and everything in-between. A large number of Jews maintain strong roots in the Middle East (from where all Jews originally came) and can trace their ancestry back almost to biblical times. Others left their ancient homeland with the earliest migrations, even before the first centuries of the Common Era. They settled in Egypt, Iraq, Iran, Ethiopia, and India where they have long histories and adapted many of the practices and languages of their host cultures. Even their physical characteristics have come to resemble those of the native population.

Still other Jews trace their cultural heritage to the many different regions of Europe where they began settling even before the fifth century C.E. Each of these groups also has its own unique history, culture, and language. We may agree that once, before their expulsion from ancient Israel some 2,000 years ago, Jews were one ethnic group. But that would still not include the many people from all lands who, over the centuries, have converted to Judaism and whose descendents are Jewish.

Another possible way to define Judaism is as a common belief, but this, by itself, also proves to be problematic. For example, if Judaism is only a religion and Jews are simply those who practice that religion, then we might assume that if a Jew converted, he would then be defined by his new faith, as a Christian or a Muslim or a Buddhist. This, however, is rarely true.

It is not unusual for Jews, even if they do convert, to be considered Jewish both by others outside Judaism and by those within it. The Jews in Spain and Portugal were forced to become Christians during a period of persecution from the fourteenth to sixteenth centuries. Nevertheless, 500 years later, the descendents of those Jews are often still considered Jewish by their non-Jewish neighbors. And Jews who willingly converted to Christianity during the Nazi era to escape the antisemitic decrees before and during World War II were arrested and killed despite their new religion. To complicate matters still further, some Jews are not religious and often deny a belief in God, and yet they consider themselves Jewish and are accepted as Jews by others.

Faced with all these inconsistencies, some Jews have defined Judaism as a shared culture. It is a culture that includes holidays, common historical memories, a language, a variety of folkways, and a set of shared assumptions and reactions. This definition could include religion but could also embrace those who are not religious but still feel tied to Judaism and the Jewish people. In answer to the eternal question, Who is a Jew? one twentieth-century philosopher, Abraham Joshua Heschel, replied: A Jew is "a person who knows how to recall and to keep alive what is holy in our people's past, and to cherish the promise and the vision of redemption in the days to come."[1] Mordecai Kaplan, another twentieth-century philosopher, took this concept one step further. He called Judaism a civilization.[2]

This definition can best be understood by comparing Jewish culture to the culture of any large, modern nation. In the United States, for example, citizens are not defined by any single ethnic group. It is a multi-ethnic society, and many groups retain their language of origin in addition to English. A small number never learn much English but are still considered Americans. Religious beliefs vary and people are free to believe what they want—or to have no faith. Loyalty to the country also runs the gamut in the United States. There are those who are fiercely patriotic and others who are indifferent and even live most of their lives abroad. Likewise, American history, beginning with the Revolutionary War, is not the history of the majority of today's Americans who came to these shores long after that war was fought. Yet with all these differences there is something that ties Americans together, wherever they live, and makes them feel American.

The same is true for Jews. Each individual Jew may define Judaism differently and may stress any single aspect of it or any combination: religion, nationality, ethnicity, history, and culture.

This book attempts to explain those aspects of Judaism in all their complexity and diversity. Beginning with the basic concepts of God and peoplehood, the reader will move through the centuries to an examination of the changing philosophies and practices of the Jews up to our own time. This book also addresses some of the less understood and more controversial tenets of Judaism such as food prohibitions, the idea of the Chosen People, and the Jews' continuing allegiance to Israel.

All attempts have been made to present each subgroup and each set of ideas evenhandedly, without judging them. In this way, the student will begin to understand not only the details, but also the scope of Judaism: a large umbrella that covers a diverse assortment of people and a wide variety of beliefs.

NOTES

1. Reuven Kimelman, "Abraham Joshua Heschel: Our Generation's Teacher," in *Melton Journal* 15 (Winter, 1983), pp. 3, 23f.

2. Mordecai M. Kaplan is the founder of the Reconstructionist movement in the United States. His book *Judaism as a Civilisation* (1934; reprint, Philadelphia: Jewish Publication Society, 1994) explains this broad definition.

TIMELINE

c. 1900–1800 B.C.E.	Abraham and Sarah, the founding parents of the 12 tribes of Israel, travel South into Canaan.
c. 1280	Exodus from Egypt.
c. 1240	The 12 tribes of Israel settle in Canaan, the land promised to them by God.
c. 1020–1004	Israel gets a king; Saul reigns as the first king of Israel.
c. 1004–965	King David's reign.
c. 965–928	King Solomon reigns; the Holy Temple is built.
928	The land of Israel is divided into two parts: Israel and Judah.
722	Destruction of Israel; Exile of the 10 northern tribes.
586	King Nebuchadnezzar destroys Judah; destruction of the Temple and exile to Babylonia.
538	Some Jews allowed to return from Babylonia and begin to rebuild the Temple.
444	Nehemiah arrives in Judah to help rebuild the country. Ezra, a great religious leader, follows him.
332	Alexander the Great conquers the land of Israel; it becomes part of a new Hellenistic Empire.

323	Death of Alexander the Great and the division of his Empire.
165	The Jewish uprising led by the Maccabees; beginning of the Hasmonean Empire.
63	End of Hasmonean Empire, beginning of Roman influence.
37	Herod I is appointed king by the Romans.
30 C.E.	Death of Jesus of Nazareth and the beginning of Christianity.
68–70	Destruction of Jerusalem by the Romans.
132–135	Simon Bar Kokhba leads a final rebellion against Rome and rules briefly; after three years, he is defeated by the Romans.
200	The Mishnah, the first book of commentary on biblical law, is completed.
313	Christianity becomes an accepted religion in the Roman Empire.
381	Christianity becomes the only legal religion of the Roman Empire.
c. 350–400	The Palestinian Talmud, containing a partial commentary on the Mishnah, is closed.
406–476	Germanic tribes invade the Roman Empire; Rome falls.
c. 500–540	The Babylonian Talmud, a more complete commentary on the Mishnah, is closed.
589	Beginning of the period of the gaonim, head scholars of the Jewish academies in Babylonia.
632	Death of Muhammad, the founder of the Muslim religion, and the beginnings of Islam.
661	The first Islamic Empire is established; the Middle East is ruled by the Muslims.
711	Muslims conquer Spain.
800	King Charlemagne is crowned Emperor of the Holy Roman Empire and rules most of northern Europe; Charlemagne invites the Jews in to trade.

900–1000	Organized Jewish communities are established in northern Europe.
960–1028	R. Gershom, "Light of the Exile," the first great European sage.
1030	Hai, the last gaon, dies; The Babylonian gaonate comes to an end.
1040–1105	R. Solomon ben Isaac (Rashi), the greatest commentator, explains the Bible and Talmud for European Jews.
1066	Jews enter England with William the Conqueror.
1096	The First Crusade; Christians march across Europe to capture the land of Israel from Muslim rule; several thousand European Jews are killed.
1099	Jerusalem is captured by the Crusaders.
1135–1204	R. Moses ben Maimon (Maimonides), a great sage of Egypt and one of the most influential scholars in Judaism.
1147–1149	Second Crusade.
1215	Church Council rules that European Jews must wear a badge to identify themselves.
1233	Inquisition first established in Europe for persons accused of heresy.
1242	Talmud is burned in Paris.
1290	Expulsion of the Jews from England.
1306	Expulsion of the Jews from northern France.
1453	The Rise of the Ottoman Empire, a new haven for the Jews of Europe; more Jews return to the land of Israel, now ruled by the Ottoman Turks.
1475	Beginning of Hebrew printing.
1480	The Inquisition is established in Spain to find and eliminate nonorthodox practice in the Catholic Church.
1492	Granada, the last Muslim stronghold in Spain, is conquered by the Catholics; expulsion of the Jews from Spain; Christopher Columbus arrives in the New World.

1493	The *Shulhan Arukh* by Joseph Caro is published.
1497	The forced conversion of all Portuguese Jews.
1497–1650	Thousands of secret Jews find their way out of Portugal to Amsterdam, Turkey, the land of Israel, and the New World; thousands more remain, secretly practicing Judaism.
1569–71	A gloss to the *Shulhan Arukh* is published by Moses Isserles, differentiating certain traditions of Ashkenazi (German) Jews from Sephardi (Spanish/Portuguese) Jews.
1580	Growth of a strong Jewish community in Eastern Europe; ruled by a Jewish Council of the Four Lands.
1648–1649	Chmielnicki pogroms; large numbers of Jews in the Ukraine and Poland are massacred.
1654	The first Jews settle in the North American colonies (New Amsterdam).
1665	Shabbetai Zevi, a Turkish Jew, proclaims himself to be the Messiah of the Jews, then converts to Islam.
1669	Death of Shabbetai Zevi.
1700–1760	The Baal Shem Tov, an Eastern European charismatic Jew, begins to preach a new kind of Judaism; his philosophy marks the rise of Hasidism.
1729–1786	Moses Mendelssohn, a German-Jewish philosopher from Berlin, teaches "enlightened" Judaism to German Jews.
1772	Jews of eastern Poland come under Russian rule.
1791	Russia declares Jews are limited to one area of settlement (the Pale of Settlement).
1818	First Reform Temple in Hamburg, Germany.
1854	Beginning of "historical Judaism," the basis of the Conservative Movement, formed in Breslau, Germany.
1875	Hebrew Union College, the first seminary for Rabbis in the New World, is opened in Cincinnati, Ohio, to train Reform rabbis.
1876	Orthodoxy as a movement begins in Hungary and Germany.

1878	Beginning of the political antisemitic movement in Berlin.
1880–1924	Jewish immigrants from Eastern Europe come to the United States in large numbers.
1882	Jews begin returning to the land of Israel; the development of the Zionist movement.
1887	Conservative Jewish seminary opens in New York City.
1896	Theodore Herzl, a Hungarian Jew, publishes *The Jewish State;* beginning of political Zionism.
1902	Union of Orthodox Rabbis of the United States and Canada founded.
1903–1906	Pogroms in Russia; more Jews leave for the land of Israel.
1914–1918	World War I; Turkey fights with Germany and loses.
1917	The Middle East is removed from Turkish rule and transferred to England as a protectorate; The Balfour Declaration: England promises a homeland for the Jews in Palestine.
1922	Founding of the Society for the Advancement of Judaism in the United States and the beginning of the Reconstructionist movement.
1924	McCarran-Walter Act closes immigration to the United States.
1925–1927	Adolf Hitler's manifesto, *Mein Kampf,* is published in Germany.
1938	*Kristallnacht,* the "night of broken glass" marks the official beginning of Jewish persecution in Germany; synagogues and Jewish establishments are burned.
1939	Poland is attacked by Germany on September 1; beginning of World War II.
1945	Germany and Japan surrender; end of World War II; six million European Jews have been murdered by Nazis and their supporters.
1947	Israel is granted independence by the United Nations; recognized by both Russia and the United States.

1948	British troops pull out of Israel on May 14; Jews declare an independent state and are immediately attacked by surrounding Arab nations.
1948–1960	Ingathering of Jewish exiles; Jews expelled from Arab lands.
1967	Six-Day War; Israel now controls the West Bank and Gaza.
1972	First woman rabbi ordained in the United States.
1973	Yom Kippur War; Egypt accepts a peace treaty with Israel.
1982	Israel attacks Lebanon.
1984	The Conservative movement agrees to ordain women rabbis.
1987	The first Intifada (popular rebellion) of Palestinian Arabs.
1992	500th anniversary of the expulsion of Jews from Spain; crypto-Jews begin openly returning to Judaism.
1995-present	Reemergence of antisemitism in Europe.
1998	Clinton peace plan between Israel and the Palestinians is presented to Prime Minister Barak of Israel and Palestinian leader, Yassir Arafat at Camp David; it fails when Arafat refuses terms; Intifada resumes.
2001	Arab terrorists crash planes into the Pentagon and the World Trade Center in New York, causing the twin towers to collapse. U.S. forces attack Afghanistan and drive out extreme Muslim rulers.
2003	U.S. forces bomb and conquer Iraq and topple dictator Saddam Hussein; United States publicly supports Israel's struggle against terrorism.
2004	European powers insist that Iraqi problem cannot be settled unless peace is achieved between Israel and the Palestinians.

1

HISTORY OF FOUNDATION

The earliest foundations of Judaism are known only from biblical stories. This chapter introduces some of those stories, showing the roots of the children of Israel beginning with their earliest ancestors, Abraham and Sarah. The chapter also traces the development of the people from a family to a tribe, to 12 tribes, and finally to a nation. When the political nation of Israel was destroyed, however, the people did not disappear from history as had so many others. By using their law and their texts as a unifying force, Jews transformed themselves into a world religion.

BIBLICAL FOUNDATIONS

God's First Promise to Abraham

Judaism has its earliest beginnings in the biblical story of Abraham and Sarah. According to this story, Abraham was the first man to believe in a single God. He was part of a family originally from Ur of the Chaldees, the area that lies between the Tigris and Euphrates Rivers called the Fertile Crescent. Together with his father, Terah, and other family members, Abraham journeyed southward to the land of Harran. In Harran, Terah died.

It was then that God revealed himself to Abraham, saying: "Go forth from your native land and from your father's house to the land that I will show you. I will make of you a great nation and I will bless you" (Genesis 12:1–2).[1] Abraham took his wife Sarah and his nephew Lot and left his family, traveling into the land of Canaan, where he settled. There is no definitive date for this occurrence and no historical evidence of Abraham or his family. Based on descriptions of the culture in the biblical text, however, scholars estimate that Abraham and Sarah, or others like them, must have lived sometime between 1900 and 1800 B.C.E. (before the Common Era).[2]

Abraham and the Biblical Family Line

When Sarah and Abraham were quite old, Sarah bore one son, Isaac. Isaac married Rebecca, a young woman from the household of Abraham's brother, the branch of the family that had remained in Harran.

Rebecca and Isaac had twin sons, Esau and Jacob. Although Esau was technically the firstborn of the twins and was entitled to inherit his father's lands and be the head of the family, God had told Rebecca that Jacob was destined to succeed his father. Rebecca made sure this would happen by helping Jacob to trick Isaac. Following his mother's instructions, Jacob posed as Esau and went in to his dying father to ask for his blessing. Isaac was blind, and, thinking Jacob was Esau, he gave him the blessing of the firstborn. As a result, Esau was angry and Jacob was forced to flee. He ran north, back to Harran where the family had its roots, and stayed in the household of his uncle Laban.

When Jacob first arrived in Harran, he caught sight of a young woman watering her flocks and fell in love with her. Her name was Rachel and she was Laban's younger daughter. When he arrived at Laban's house, he asked for her hand in marriage. Laban agreed on condition that Jacob work for him for seven years. His seven years of labor would be considered the bride price for Laban's daughter. In ancient times, it was customary for a man to pay in money, goods, or services to the bride's family before the marriage. This was not a purchase; rather it was an acknowledgment that the woman was a valuable asset to her birth family. The bride price was compensation for the loss of the family's daughter. But after Jacob worked for seven years, Laban tricked him by sending Rachel's older sister, Leah, into the wedding tent. When Jacob became angry, Laban explained that it was the custom in their land for the oldest daughter to be married first. He promised him Rachel, too, if Jacob would remain and work for another seven years. Jacob agreed and both sisters became his wives.

After 14 years in service to his father-in-law, Jacob decided to return to the land of his fathers and claim his inheritance. He gathered his en-

Art Nouveau print of Jacob wrestling with the Angel. Courtesy of the Library of the Jewish Theological Seminary.

tire household, including his wives, his children, and his servants, and left Harran. When he came into Canaan, he knew that he had to make peace with his brother Esau before he could resettle on his father's lands. Jacob sent messengers ahead to tell Esau that he was coming, but he worried that his brother might still be angry and would harm his family. He sent them all to a place of safety and stayed alone to wait for Esau.

That night, Jacob had a dream in which he wrestled with a stranger. When the sun rose, Jacob's hip was injured but neither he nor the stranger had clearly won the fight. The stranger said, "Let me go for dawn is breaking." But Jacob, apparently sensing this was no ordinary man, refused to let him leave until he received a blessing from the stranger. The stranger answered, "Your name shall no longer be Jacob, but Israel, for you have striven with beings divine and human and have prevailed" (Genesis 32: 26–29).

In the early history of ancient Israel, this dream was accepted as a sign from God. It affirmed that Jacob had inherited the original promise made to his grandfather Abraham—that he would become a great nation. And in fact, Jacob, now called Israel, eventually fathered 12 sons and 1 daughter from four different women. These 12 sons became the 12 tribes of Israel.

Egypt and the Exodus Back to the Promised Land

Genesis, the first book of the Hebrew Bible, is filled with stories about Abraham and Sarah, Isaac and Rebecca, and Jacob, Rachel, and Leah, the founders of the Jewish people, as well as their children. One of the last stories in Genesis tells of the resentment directed to Rachel's firstborn son, Joseph. Joseph was Jacob's favorite child and his half brothers were jealous of him. To take revenge on Joseph, they sold him into slavery. But Joseph, a talented young man, did not remain a slave for long. By means of his understanding of dreams, loyalty, and outstanding character, Joseph soon became one of the top officials in Egypt. That is how he came to be in a position to help his brothers when they traveled to Egypt to buy food during a famine.

When the brothers recognized each other and were reconciled, Joseph asked them to come down to Egypt with their father so they would not be hungry. Jacob's entire family, including children and grandchildren, settled in Egypt. Protected by Joseph and his friends in the government, they grew numerous and prospered. Many years passed. The 12 brothers all died, but their descendants remained and expanded into tribes, separate but united by the same ancestors: Abraham, Isaac, and Jacob (or Israel).

After many generations, the dynasty in Egypt changed, and the new rulers forgot about Joseph and no longer felt any allegiance to his people who served their own God and did not follow Egyptian ways. The new Pharaoh enslaved the children of Israel (now referred to as "the Hebrews") and kept them in bondage to build the new cities of Pithom and Ramses. In addition, to prevent the Hebrews from becoming too numerous, the Pharaoh issued a decree that any male child born to the Hebrews was to be killed.

It was in Egypt, in this climate of oppression, that a new leader of the Israelites arose. His name was Moses, from the tribe of Levi (one of Jacob's 12 sons). The biblical legend (Exodus 2) tells that the Pharaoh's daughter, Bithia, found him floating on the Nile River in a basket made of reeds. She immediately arranged for a nurse to care for him, and that nurse was Moses's own mother, Yoheved. In this way, Moses was raised in the palace but knew his origins.

When Moses grew older and saw how his people were mistreated, he lost his temper and killed one of the Egyptian overseers. Frightened that he would be punished for his crime, he ran away to the land of Midian. In Midian, he married a woman named Tzipporah.

It was in Midian that God once again revealed himself, this time in a burning bush that was not consumed. As he stared at the bush, Moses heard a voice saying, "I am the God of your fathers, the God of Abraham, Isaac and Jacob" (Exodus 3:6). God told Moses that he must return to Egypt to rescue his people from slavery and lead them back to the land that had been promised to Abraham and his descendants.

Although Moses doubted his own ability, God promised to help him, assuring him that Moses's older brother Aaron would be there with him to confront the Pharaoh. When the Pharaoh refused to release the Hebrews, God inflicted a series of 10 plagues on the Egyptians. Finally, after the Egyptian people had experienced much suffering, the Israelites, together with a "mixed multitude" (Exodus 12:38) of other peoples, were allowed to leave Egypt. This event and those that followed immediately after are still remembered in the Jewish holiday of Passover. Again, no definitive date is known for this event, and, outside of the Bible, there is no historical report of it. But basing their estimates on the text itself and what they know from archaeology, biblical historians place the Exodus from Egypt in approximately 1280 B.C.E., or about 600 to 700 years after Abraham and Sarah lived.

The story of how the children of Israel crossed the sea and then wandered in the desert for 40 years is well known. It can be found in detail in Exodus, the second book of the Hebrew Bible. Exodus ends with the Israelites receiving the Ten Commandments and building a tabernacle to hold them.

After many more years of wandering, the Hebrews finally crossed over the Jordan River into the Promised Land. By this time, a whole new generation had arisen that had not experienced slavery. Moses himself was not permitted to enter the land. After allotting portions of the Promised Land to each of the tribes, he died outside its boundaries.

Moses remains a seminal figure in the establishment of the Jewish people and their beliefs, having led the Israelites out of Egypt and through the desert. It was Moses alone who went up to Mount Sinai to receive the Ten Commandments, engraved them on stone tablets, and brought them down to the people. During those 40 years of wandering, Moses judged the Israelites and taught them the laws of God. Before he died, he appointed Joshua as his successor.

Uniting the Tribes

Joshua was the first of many judges and prophets who led Israel after Moses's death. Once the Israelites arrived in the land of Canaan, these leaders helped to defeat the local tribes and were instrumental in establishing a government. But the 12 tribes of Israel were still a loose confederation, not yet united.

Eventually, the people asked for a king to lead them so that they could be like other nations. Although the prophet Samuel warned against a king, he finally succumbed to the urgings of the Israelites and Saul was appointed the first ruler. He was succeeded by David, the most popular and beloved of all the Kings of Israel, and then by David's son, Solomon.

During most of the reign of Saul, approximately 1020 to 1004 B.C.E., the Israelites were engaged in war against the Philistines, a tribe located on the Mediterranean Coast, near present-day Ashkelon.[3] When David succeeded as king, the Philistines were finally defeated and Jerusalem was established as the capital city and the place where the holy tablets of the Ten Commandments would be kept. David's reign lasted for almost 40 years, until 965 B.C.E.. Under David's son, Solomon (965–928 B.C.E.), the Temple was built in Jerusalem and was designated as a place to serve and honor God, mainly by animal sacrifice. All these events were recorded in the biblical books Samuel I and II, and Kings I.

The tribe of Levi, Moses's tribe, was responsible for the service in the Holy Temple and became an official, hereditary priesthood. The High Priest, the most important man in the early religion of the Israelites, was to be a direct descendant of Moses's older brother, Aaron. This elite group of priests was referred to as *Kohanim* (the Hebrew plural word for priest, *kohen*), a category that still exists today and is passed down from father to son.[4]

Exile of the 10 Northern Tribes

In 928 B.C.E., shortly after King Solomon died, the 12 tribes of Israel split into two nations. The 10 tribes living in the north called themselves Israel. They established a separate government and chose their own king. The remaining two tribes, Judah and Benjamin, formed the smaller country of Judah, keeping Jerusalem as their capital.

When the Assyrians conquered Israel in 722 B.C.E., they exiled much of the original population and those 10 tribes were scattered throughout other nations and became assimilated. They are remembered as the lost tribes of Israel.[5] Once these tribes disappeared, the main source of Judaism and the Jewish people was the tiny land of Judah and its capital city, Jerusalem.

The Exile to Babylonia and the Beginning of the Diaspora ⸺

Because of its crucial place ~~at~~ (since) the crossroads of the Middle East, Judah was attacked often and suffered many setbacks. Finally, in 586 B.C.E., the powerful King Nebuchadnezzar of Babylonia conquered Judah. The walls of Jerusalem were breached, the city and the Temple were burned, and a large portion of the inhabitants were exiled to Babylonia (present-day Iraq).

Initially, the people of Judah were ~~devastated~~ told to leave their homeland and their center of worship in Jerusalem. They never replaced the Holy Temple with a new one in Babylonia, but they did build the first synagogues (a Greek word that means "meeting house"), and organized themselves into a community there. In subsequent generations, the children of Israel did so well in Babylonia that in 537 B.C.E., when Persia conquered Babylonia and the new Persian king, Cyrus, declared that he would allow the Israelites to return to their homeland, many opted to remain. The Babylonian Jewish community eventually became a great center for Judaism, and its establishment marked the beginning of the Diaspora.

Those who returned to Judah found the holy places in ruins, the remaining population depressed, ~~and Jerusalem desolate~~. But they slowly rebuilt both the Temple and the city, repopulated their land, and set up an independent government.

The Rule of the Maccabees

The land of Judah maintained its independence for several generations after the return from exile, but its government was weak. Eventually, tiny Judah fell prey first to the military prowess of Alexander the Great in 332 B.C.E. and, after Alexander's death 10 years later, to the might of the Hellenistic-Greek Empire.[6]

Judah did become independent once again for a brief time under the rule of the Maccabees. In 165 B.C.E., this family organized a rebellion against Greek rule and its harsh insistence on the Greek religion, and they succeeded in driving out the Greek/Syrian kings. Their victory is still remembered today with the holiday of Hanukkah, and their struggles are told in the apocryphal books Maccabees I and II.

Late Medieval German rendering of the Maccabees recapturing the
Holy Temple and destroying the idols. Courtesy of the Library of the
Jewish Theological Seminary.

Within a few generations, however, the Maccabean kingdom of Judah,
suffering from a combination of weak leaders and corruption, was taken
over by Rome. At first, Rome set up puppet governments to do its bid-
ding, but finally took control itself. The inhabitants resisted and in a final
battle, in 68–70 c.e., Jerusalem was destroyed, the Holy Temple once again
burned to the ground, and the bulk of the population sent into exile.[7]

During this terrible and destructive war, a large portion of the people of
Judah fled. Some went to Babylonia; others went south to Egypt or to places
farther afield. A fairly large group was captured by the Romans and taken
to Rome as slaves, marking one of the earliest documented appearances
of Jews in Europe. This Roman victory is depicted on the famous Arch of
Titus, still standing in Rome, amidst the ruins of the Roman Forum. By informal tradition, Jews visiting the area never walk under the Arch.

THE BEGINNING OF RABBINIC JUDAISM

The Oral Tradition

Even before the second century b.c.e., academies of learning had been
established in the land of Israel. In these academies, scholars studied the
scrolls of the Bible and analyzed the law, trying to understand what God
wanted from the people. Often these discussions were not based solely

on biblical texts, but also on oral law, popular interpretations of biblical law and custom. It was called oral law because it had never been written down. Instead, the traditions were memorized and passed from generation to generation. At some point during the rule of the Maccabees, a group of scholars, the Pharisees, made the decision to write down the oral law.

Johanan ben Zakkai and the Beginning of Rabbinic Judaism

When the Romans exiled the inhabitants of Judah (or Judea, as it was now called) in 68–70 C.E., the people could neither take the Holy Temple with them nor have their own ruler, but they could take their Bible and their written law. A famous legend tells us that as Jerusalem lay under siege, one of the greatest scholars of the city, a man named Johanan ben Zakkai, was secretly smuggled out in a coffin. He established a new academy in a small city called Jabneh. From Jabneh, he continued the teachings of the sages, thus ensuring that the laws of the people would be followed even though Jerusalem and the Holy Temple were destroyed.[8]

In the academy at Jabneh—and eventually in other academies established outside the boundaries of the old Judean state—the laws contained in the Torah, the first five books of the Hebrew Bible, were studied and taught. Over the course of 300 years, they were written down. When a final

Bas-relief on the Arch of Titus shows the Roman soldiers carrying off the golden menorah from the Holy Temple in Jerusalem during the conquest of Judea in 70 C.E. The arch still stands in Rome, in the ancient Roman Forum. Courtesy of the author.

rebellion against Rome in 132–134 C.E. failed and immigration to other lands increased, this decision to write down the oral law proved vital for the survival of the Jewish people.

The Mishnah

Once completed, the centuries-old oral law was organized into a series of six books called the Mishnah, a word that means "teachings." The Mishnah was compiled and finalized in the year 200 C.E. by one of the great scholars of the law, Judah haNasi (the Patriarch). From then on, students of the law did not need to depend on a great teacher but could consult the Mishnah when they needed an answer about proper practices or traditions.

The Academies of Babylonia and Palestine

Eventually, three academies emerged as the most important centers for study. One was in the land of Israel, the historic Jewish homeland now ruled by Rome, but the other two were in Babylonia, home to the largest and most powerful Jewish community. It is at this point in history, when the children of Israel were no longer an independent nation, that the people of Judea came to be called Jews. With no political center or ruler of their own, Jews turned to their scholars for guidance; and Judaism, as a religion and a way of life, was born.

THE ESTABLISHMENT AND SPREAD OF JEWISH LAW

The Sages of the Talmud

Even after the Mishnah was closed, scholars in the great academies continued to study and discuss the law so that it would remain relevant. Their disciples wrote down the conversations of their teachers and recorded their conclusions. When these disciples became sages in their turn, others wrote down their words. In this way, a new collection of law and interpretation of law was built up, generation by generation and layer by layer. Finally, at the end of the sixth century C.E., it was all edited and closed.

This collection of law and legend, and of stories about the great scholars and their disciples, was organized according to the same categories as the Mishnah and written as a gloss, a series of comments and explanations added either in the margins of the original text or in between the lines, as was the case for the Mishnah. This elaborate gloss was called Gemara from the root *gamar*, "to finish." Together, the Mishnah and the Gemara became known as the Talmud, a word from the Hebrew root word *lamad*, "to study or learn." Gradually, the many volumes of the Talmud became increasingly important and were accepted as the standard text for Jews.

The Gaonim

As Jews traveled farther and farther away from their old homeland, they looked to the sages of the academies to help them understand and maintain Jewish practices. Although the academy in the land of Israel had stopped functioning in the year 400 C.E., the two Babylonian academies were stronger than ever. The scholars chosen to head these academies were referred to as *gaonim* (plural for *gaon*), an honorary title roughly equivalent to "Excellency," and were respected and honored as the intellectual leaders of world Jewry.[9]

Heads of individual communities in North Africa, Asia, and Europe frequently sent letters to the *gaon* of one or the other of the academies asking for advice. Their questions ranged from the proper ways to celebrate holidays, to the rules to follow for betrothal, marriage, and divorce; from the order of the prayers during morning and evening services, to how Jews should conduct themselves in business dealings. The *gaonim* consulted the Talmud and sent answers to every question. In this way, the standards set out in the Talmud by the sages spread throughout the Diaspora.

The Development of Local Scholars and Academies

Eventually, the many volumes of the Talmud were copied and became more accessible. By the late Middle Ages, new Jewish communities throughout Europe and North Africa had obtained their own copies of the Talmud and had their own sages to explain and interpret the law. This made the *gaonim* unnecessary and by the end of the eleventh century, that institution ceased to function. The Talmud maintained its importance for all Jews, though, and became the definitive guide for both Jewish communities and individuals.

As times changed, scholars explained and reevaluated Talmudic laws and opinions, building new law on top of the old. This process continues today and forms the core of Jewish religious practices.

NOTES

1. This and all other biblical quotes come from *The Torah: The Five Books of Moses*, 2nd ed. (Philadelphia: Jewish Publication Society, 1977).

2. John Bright, *A History of Israel*, 2nd ed. (Philadelphia: Westminster Press, 1972), pp. 76–85.

3. This and all other dates of reigning kings are approximate, as there is little archaeological evidence directly linked to these kings.

4. Scientists who study DNA have learned to verify whether a person is a *kohen* by tracing common genetic markers.

5. Several groups, even today, trace their ancestry back to those tribes. A theory that arose in seventeenth-century England suggested that Native American Indians were from the 10 lost tribes. A small group of Japanese people believe they are descended from one of those lost tribes, and several groups of Africans also make this claim. Although there may be truth to some of these beliefs, there is no clear proof.

6. Victor Tcherikover, *Hellenistic Civilisation and the Jews*, trans. S. Applebaum (New York: Atheneum, 1977), pp. 42–89.

7. Flavius Josephus, *The Complete Works of Josephus: Jewish War* and *Jewish Antiquities* (Cambridge, Mass.: Harvard University Press, 1925), retells the story of the Maccabean, or Hasmonean, Dynasty, the events leading up to the war with the Romans, and details of the war. Josephus lived through many of these events himself.

8. Jacob Neusner, *There We Sat Down: Talmudic Judaism in the Making* (New York: K'tav, 1972), pp. 36–38.

9. Solomon Grayzel, *A History of the Jews from the Babylonian Exile to the Present*, book 2, chapter 3, "The Babylonian Community," chapter 4, "The Sea of Learning," chapter 6, "Geonic Achievements" (Philadelphia: The Jewish Publication Society, 1947; reprint 1968).

2

TEXTS AND MAJOR TENETS

Many texts are important to Judaism, but first among them is the Hebrew Bible, the basis of Jewish law. All other major books were written to explain, expand, or help to adapt biblical law to changing times. The overriding theme of the Bible is the centrality of God, but individual laws concentrate on personal behavior and the functioning of a just society. Subsequent books, written over the course of centuries, enlarge on these ideas and give specific expression to the basic beliefs (tenets) of Judaism. These beliefs include faith in a Messiah, and in a "world to come" after death; the importance of the land of Israel, even for Jews living far from that land; and a sense of responsibility by individual Jews and Jewish communities to help each other.

THE HEBREW BIBLE

The Jews are known as "the people of the book" for good reasons. For thousands of years, their holy texts have been a portable homeland, the hub of the giant wheel of Judaism. Jewish books were instrumental in keeping the children of Israel together after they lost their geographical center and scattered throughout the world. Yet the expression "people of the book," originally coined by the early Muslims, did not refer to all the volumes of law books written by Jewish scholars, but only to the Bible. And indeed, despite all the books that have been written to explain it, the Hebrew Bible itself has remained the single work that defines the Jewish people and confirms the beginning of their existence.

The Bible and Its Message

The Bible is actually a library in itself. It consists of three parts: the Torah, the Prophets (Nevi'im), and the Writings (Ketuvim). The first letters in each of these words are assembled to create an acronym: Tanakh. The word Tanakh refers to the complete collection of biblical books.

The first and most important part of the Tanakh is the Torah, called the Pentateuch in Greek. It consists of five separate books: Genesis, Exodus, Leviticus, Numbers, and Deuteronomy. Often referred to as "the Five Books of Moses," because according to Jewish tradition, they were written down by Moses himself, these books tell the story of the earliest beginnings of the Jewish people and lay out the law that God gave to them.

Although the five books of the Pentateuch are filled with the stories of men and women, God is the prime actor in the biblical narrative. The overriding concept that the Hebrew Bible offers is that God intervenes in the world of human beings and wants people to behave according to the laws of righteousness.

Justice and Fairness as the Basis for Israelite Society

Not only does the Bible assert that God oversees the activities of all humans, but God cares especially for the people of Israel. It is to Israel alone that God has given the law so that they can conduct themselves justly and fairly. The book of Deuteronomy proclaims: "Justice, justice shall you pursue," (Deuteronomy 16:20). When Israel followed the ways of justice, God was pleased. When Israel sinned (as, according to the biblical stories, they often did), God was displeased and punished them.

The ideal of justice is reflected not only in the Torah but also in the books of Kings and the Prophets. Hosea, an Israelite prophet, wrote "Practice goodness and justice and constantly return to your God" (Hosea 12: 7) and Amos, another prophet of Israel, warned: "Hate evil and love good, and establish justice in the gate" (Amos 5:15).

Israel as a Holy and Pure People

The Ten Commandments, found in the book of Exodus and again in the book of Deuteronomy, form the core of the just laws that the children of Israel were obligated to follow. Other biblical rulings, especially those outlined in Leviticus, the third book of the Torah, give very specific details concerning day-to-day life. The idea behind many of these laws is that the Israelites must keep themselves ritually pure and holy. One of the ways they can do this is by avoiding contact with anything or anyone that is unclean. This might include someone who has a disease, an infection with running sores, or an issue of blood. Human corpses and carcasses of dead animals are also unclean. A person who comes in contact with any of these must purify him/herself in water.

Food and the Laws of *Kashrut*

Another way of remaining holy is by abstaining from foods that are forbidden. No clear reason is given for these rulings, but they form the basis of the Jewish laws of *kashrut* (ritual fitness), still followed closely by many Jews today. According to these laws, all vegetables, nuts, and fruits are permitted, but only specific forms of meat and fish. The foods that the Bible allows include all land animals that chew their cud and have a cloven hoof, all water animals that have fins and scales, and all birds except birds of prey. Dairy products are allowed, but only from kosher animals. The dietary laws stipulate that even permitted animals were to be treated with kindness and killed humanely. Animals that had met a violent death were not to be eaten.

"Do not boil a kid in its mother's milk," is a ruling repeated in three different places in the Bible.[1] This is the basis for the separation of milk and meat, another tenet that has come down through the ages. This ruling suggests that consideration should be given even to animals that are raised solely for their food. For the same reason, the Torah demands that before removing the eggs from a nest, the mother bird be chased away so she will not have to watch her eggs being taken (Leviticus 17:13).[2]

An interesting food prohibition among the Israelites was the law forbidding them to eat the sciatic nerve found in the hindquarter of animals, even kosher animals. This limitation was explained as a remembrance of Jacob, one of the founding fathers of Israel, whose thigh was injured when he struggled with the angel (see also Chapter 1). Although this "sinew of the thigh-vein" may be removed and the hindquarter eaten, removal is difficult and time-consuming.[3] For this reason observant Jews in the United States and Canada eat only the front part of the animal. In Israel, often the entire animal is prepared by butchers and considered kosher.

Other Biblical Laws

A third important category of law included in the Bible is tort law, or the laws of personal injury. For example, if an animal that one owns damages or destroys someone else's property, or injures another person, the law insists that the owner of the animal must pay for the damage. Likewise, if a person injures or wrongs another, restitution must be made. Many such examples are given in the Bible, with explanations about how each should be handled so that both parties are treated justly.

The Talmud

Because of the importance of the Bible as a book of laws, subsequent generations attempted to adapt biblical law to a changing society. The biggest change for Jews was, of course, the loss of their land. Once Jews lived under non-Jewish governments, they could no longer follow some laws, especially those related to the land and to the rituals surrounding the Holy Temple in Jerusalem.

Understanding that reality, the sages, now living in communities con-

Typical page of the Talmud with Rashi's commentary. Courtesy of the Library of the Jewish Theological Seminary.

trolled by non-Jews, reinterpreted the law and adapted it to these new cir-cumstances. That effort resulted in the Talmud, the second most important text in Judaism. Like the Hebrew Bible, the Talmud is also a collection, made up of many volumes. Its two basic parts, the Mishnah and the Ge-mara, were written and edited over the course of 600 years; therefore they reflect many different opinions and conclusions (see also Chapter 1). The sages did agree on most of the basic tenets, however, and these remain part of Judaism to this day. They also understood that, although Talmudic laws were to guide the spiritual life of the people, the laws of host countries could not be defied. "The law of the land is the law," they agreed.[4]

The 613 Commandments

One of the earliest attempts to sort out and understand biblical law resulted in counting out the number of commandments (*mitzvot* in He-brew) given in the Hebrew Bible. The conclusion was that "six hundred and thirteen commandments were revealed to Moses on Mount Sinai."[5] Of these 613, 365 were prohibitions, or negative commandments. Negative commandments stipulated the things that the children of Israel must not do. They ranged from major prohibitions, such as not worshipping other gods, not committing murder, and not perpetrating injustice, to the small-est practicalities. Among the lesser, more specific prohibitions was a rul-ing forbidding the king from accumulating an excessive number of wives or wealth. Other negative commandments warned soldiers not to destroy fruit trees, even in times of war, and forbade agricultural workers from tak-ing more fruit than they could eat during their working day.[6]

The other 248 commandments are mandates, or positive commands. These encompass a variety of things a Jew is obligated to do. Jews are man-dated to believe in the existence of a single God, to rest on the Sabbath, to restore stolen property to its owner, and to destroy the practice of idolatry. Stipulations about how the priests are to offer sacrifices in the Holy Temple are also part of the positive commandments, as are details of how to cel-ebrate festivals.

The Differing Obligations of Men and Women

All Jewish men and women have an obligation to follow the negative commandments in their entirety, but the Talmudic sages divided the posi-tive commandments into two separate categories. The first category in-cludes those that can be performed at any time. For example, believing in

God, paying tithes (10% of one's income) to the Holy Temple, resting on the Sabbath and reciting blessings when one eats are either ongoing or can be performed at any time of the day or night. For these, women and men have an equal obligation.

The rest of the positive mandates must be performed at specific times of day. Reciting the morning and evening prayers and performing most of the rituals associated with the holidays and festivals of the Jewish calendar fall into the second category. These positive, "time-bound" commandments are not obligatory for women. Studying the law was also considered a time-bound *mitzvah* that excluded most women.[7]

Several different reasons for this exclusion were posited by the early sages, as well as by the rabbis who came after them. The most accepted reason is that such obligations would cut into women's important work of household management and childcare. Modern feminist scholars have rejected this explanation, however, as well as several others, calling them rationalizations. They suggest that the Bible never intended to exclude women and that excusing women from these commandments made them second-class citizens within Judaism.

The Fence Around the Torah

The creative interpretation of biblical tenets, practiced by the scholars who wrote and edited the Talmud, often had the effect of altering Jewish law. This is the case in laws pertaining not only to the different obligations of women and men, but also to other categories. The laws of *kashrut* and Sabbath observance and also the rules concerning marriage and divorce are examples of how the sages adapted and ultimately transformed the original laws. The transformation often stemmed from the desire to be strict about observance and ensure that laws were not broken inadvertently. The rabbis called this "putting a fence around the Torah."

Concerning the rules of *kashrut,* the Bible simply lists the foods the Israelites are permitted to eat, stipulating clean and unclean animals, and suggesting a humane method of slaughter. It also warns against eating the meat and the milk of an animal together. To be absolutely certain that these rulings were followed, a whole series of new stipulations were suggested and later put into place. For example, to ensure that meat and milk were never mixed, even inadvertently, the sages demanded that separate dishes and utensils be used for each category of food. Nevertheless, if a mistake was made, special procedures for cleansing the utensils were to be followed. To ensure that an animal was not slaughtered improperly, the slaughter of animals had to be performed only by those specially learned in that skill. All these are Talmudic, and not biblical, laws. They were formulated, however, to make sure that biblical law remained intact.

Similar laws surround the observance of the Sabbath. Not only was the biblical prohibition against doing work on the day of rest reiterated, it was further stipulated that no one initiate any activity that might *appear* to be work. For example, one must not use tools on the Sabbath; or even pick up a tool lest someone see and think that person had been working.

Divorce law, too, was hedged with minute stipulations to ensure that no misunderstanding persisted. Although the Bible simply states that to divorce a woman, a man must give her a bill of divorcement (Deuteronomy 24:1–4), the Talmud elaborated on that rule. It explained how the bill of divorce was to be worded and executed and how it was to be presented to the wife and accepted by her. If any of these standards were not met, the divorce would not be valid.

There are many examples of such exegesis or interpretation of the Hebrew Bible. Some created more prohibitions and some fewer. When the scholars saw that a law was no longer possible, or was harmful for Jews, they made it more lenient. They explained this by quoting the Bible itself, pointing out that God gave Israel a law "to live by" and not to make living more difficult (Leviticus 18:5). In this spirit, many prohibitions and stipulations were eased to enable Jews to make a living, to avoid persecution by non-Jews in power, and especially to save a life.

Pikuah nefesh followed this ideal. The expression *pikuah nefesh*, "safeguarding human life," alludes to the fact that all things are permissible to save a human being. Sabbath laws, abstaining from forbidden foods, and vowing and keeping an oath, are important precepts, but they can all be set aside if the life of a single individual is at stake.[8]

Nonlegal Material in the Talmud

In addition to rulings, opinions, and explanations, the Talmud includes anecdotes and stories that give clues to the lives of the great sages themselves and tell of popular beliefs, morality, and customs. Details about the practice of magic, relationships between the rabbis and their wives, incidents that occurred in the house of study, and memories of great teachers long since dead are also an important part of the material found in "the sea of Talmud." Even modern scholars liken the Talmud to a sea. Another important saying about the Talmud is: "Turn it, and turn it again, for everything is within it."[9]

OTHER LAW CODES AND GLOSSES

Although the Talmud was closed by the beginning of the sixth century C.E., the process of interpreting and adapting the law did not stop. Scholars continued studying and explaining and produced a variety of new codes intended to make biblical and Talmudic rulings relevant and more easily understood. One of the early and most successful attempts was written by Solomon ben Isaac, a great sage of eleventh-centuryFrance, best known by his Hebrew acronym, Rashi (*Rav* [master or teacher]) Shlomo Yitzhaki.

Rashi's Explanations and the School of Rashi

Rashi's scholarly output was broad and made a profound impression not only on his own pupils and disciples but on the entire Jewish world. He painstakingly went over most of the books of the Bible and explained them in Hebrew, sometimes mixed with the French dialect that the Jews spoke at that time. In his comments and glosses, he analyzed and smoothed out any possible ambiguities of meaning.

Rashi also commented on most of the tractates of the Talmud, pointing out difficulties in grammar and subject matter and often explaining a particular law by using examples from contemporary life. His writings were immensely popular and by the thirteenth century, they had circulated widely. Even today, almost all editions of the Talmud are printed together with Rashi's commentary, and his corrections and explanations of Talmudic texts have been incorporated into the law.[10]

Even before Rashi's death, the next generation of scholars, including his own grandsons, were critiquing and questioning his conclusions. These twelfth- to fourteenth-century European scholars were called Tosafists from the Hebrew word *tosafot,* meaning "additions." They added to Rashi's commentaries and made some comments of their own. Although their work is not as original as Rashi's and is not as well known, it has been added to most editions of the Talmud.

Maimonides and His Code of Law

In approximately 1180, almost a full century after Rashi wrote his work, Maimonides, the Greek name of the great Jewish scholar, Moses ben Maimon, completed the *Mishneh Torah,* his explanation of the law. The *Mishneh Torah* immediately became controversial, sparking debates among Jews themselves. One of the main criticisms of this code (also known as *Yad haHazakah*, "The Strong Hand") was that Maimonides did not follow the traditional order of the Mishnah and Gemara and did not give the Talmudic sources for his conclusions. Unlike Rashi's commentary, which was a gloss, written in the margins of the Talmud and intended to be read together with it, Maimonides designed and organized his book as a replacement for the Talmud and its sometimes cumbersome deliberations. He wanted to simplify attempts at understanding the body of Jewish law and answer questions definitively rather than offering majority and minority opinions. Also unlike the Talmud, which is in Aramaic, the Mishneh Torah is written in clear and concise Hebrew and is divided into 14 parts.[11]

Despite ongoing controversy, Maimonides's work was finally accepted and today is thought of as one of the most complete and remarkable of all the law codes. Yet, none of these codes, no matter how complete and up-to-date they seemed at the time, remained completely relevant for long. In every generation, there was at least one sage who thought he could do better or could make Jewish law still clearer, easier, and more pertinent. One of these men was Jacob ben Asher.

Jacob ben Asher's "Four Rows"

Rabbi Jacob ben Asher was born in Spain but lived a good part of his life in Germany, devoting himself to study. His greatest work, *Arba'ah Turim* (translated as "The Four Rows"), was written in the fourteenth century, almost 200 years after Maimonides's *Mishneh Torah*. The *Arba'ah Turim* was Rabbi Jacob's attempt at simplifying and clarifying Talmudic law. As he himself explained: "reasoning had become faulty, controversy had increased, opinions had multiplied."[12]

The new work was designed to eliminate such problems and to clearly spell out the laws and customs that Jews had to follow. In his extensive work, comprising four volumes and approximately 1,700 chapters, he cited all the relevant Talmudic laws, as well as the opinions of the legal authorities who preceded him. Although *Arba'ah Turim* was still not definitive enough to make subsequent codification unnecessary, his work became a model for other codes.

The Shulhan Arukh

By the sixteenth century, the Jews of Europe had experienced some cataclysmic changes: Most of the Jewish population had been expelled from Western Europe, including the Jewish community of Spain, once the largest and most prosperous in the entire continent. In the face of these upheavals, Joseph Caro thought it necessary to write a new code. Although modeled after the structure of the *Arba'ah Turim,* it was more concise and similar to Maimonides's earlier code; it did not include Talmudic sources. Caro called it the *Shulhan Arukh,* the "Set Table."

The *Shulhan Arukh* was a welcome addition to all previous explanations, but there was one major problem: It reflected the laws and traditions as they were practiced by Jews from the Iberian Peninsula—Spain and Portugal. These Jews were called Sephardim from the Hebrew word for Spain and at that time, they represented a majority of all Jews. However, the *Ashkenazi* Jews, those originating in Germany and now living mainly in Eastern Europe, were unfamiliar with many of the Sephardi traditions and practices. To make the *Shulhan Arukh* relevant for the Jews of Eastern Europe, a gloss was written by the Ashkenazi scholar Moses Isserles. Called a *mappah* ("a tablecloth"), it added to the "set table," noting where Ashkenazi usage differed from the customs of the Sephardim and explaining the traditions of the Ashkenazim.

The *Shulhan Arukh,* first printed in 1493, was reprinted in Venice in 1569, along with its *mappah.* It is the last code of laws that was universally accepted by Jewish communities everywhere. Because other prominent scholars have consistently updated it over the centuries, it has remained more relevant. Many other codes have been written since then, but none has gained general acceptance among world Jewry.

THE SIDDUR, THE JEWISH PRAYER BOOK

No list of important Jewish texts would be complete without including the siddur. Siddur, literally, means "order" in Hebrew and refers to the order of daily, Sabbath, and holiday prayers. There is some evidence that prayers and psalms were recited even while the Holy Temple was functioning. After the final destruction of the Temple, however, the recitation of prayers and blessings completely replaced the priestly rituals and animal sacrifices that had been practiced before the Jews were exiled from the land of Israel.[13]

The Siddur appeared relatively late in the history of Jewish literary works and was not put into a definitive order until several hundred years after the close of the Talmud. In fact, early Talmudic statements forbade the writing down of the order of prayers. The assumption was that all prayer came from the heart. After the Talmud was closed, however, this ruling was ignored and by the eighth century c.e., prayer books were in common use.

Many siddurim (prayer books) were beautifully written in calligraphy and bound in silver. This Sabbath and holiday prayer book is from Amsterdam, printed in approximately 1785. Courtesy of Temple Israel Museum, Great Neck, New York.

Early Collections of Prayer

The first collection of prayers that has survived from those early centuries is the *Siddur Rav Amram Gaon.* It was compiled in the ninth century by Amram, head of one of the Babylonian academies, at the request of the Jewish communities of Spain. Amram's siddur gives the texts of all prayers and blessings, together with the relevant biblical or Talmudic laws, organizing them in the proper order for the entire year. Other prayer books succeeded this first one, each with small variations based on the tradition of a particular Jewish community.

Changes in the Hebrew Prayer Book

Over the centuries, certain communities have added a variety of additional readings; other communities and denominations have omitted sections of the original siddur. As the Hebrew language fell into disuse by the Jews, prayer books began to include side-by-side translations in a variety of languages. Such translations have been constantly updated as language evolved. Despite all these changes, however, the basic order of prayers has remained relatively the same (see also Chapter 4). For many modern Jews, the siddur is the only Hebrew book besides the Bible that they are likely to see and use in their lifetimes.

SOME BASIC BELIEFS

The Centrality of Torah

No matter how much individual scholars disagreed or contradicted each other on matters of law, they generally agreed on a set of basic beliefs. One of these beliefs was that the Hebrew Bible was the source of all law. They also agreed that the laws of the Bible were of vital importance to the Jewish people and, as the word of God, was binding on all Jews.

Is the Bible Literally the Word of God?

In ancient times, no one questioned that the Torah was the word of God, dictated on Mount Sinai and written down by Moses. Even the chapter that described Moses's death was believed to have been foretold by God and dictated to Moses. Although it was acknowledged that the Books of the Prophets were written by the prophets themselves, it was clear that they were also interpreting, if not repeating verbatim, the words of God. Only the third part of the Bible, the Writings, was acknowledged to have been written by human beings, usually the kings and leaders of Israel. Most of Psalms was attributed to King David; The Song of Songs and Ecclesiastes are, by tradition, the work of King Solomon; and the books of Ezra and Nehemiah were credited to those postexilic national leaders (see also Chapter 6).

Because the Bible contains so much material that forms the basis of belief for many religions, and has given the world a moral code and examples of just law and righteous behavior, people have been reluctant to challenge the premise of its God-given origins. As science continued to make inroads into Western culture, however, rationalism superseded a belief in the supernatural, and various changes in Jewish attitudes have developed concerning the Bible and its origins.

Many Jews suggest that the Torah, although not literally God's word, represents the best inspiration of human beings, an inspiration that emanates from God. This suggestion takes into account the conclusions of all the nineteenth century biblical scholars. These scholars, mostly from the German (non-Jewish) biblical school, examined and analyzed the Pentateuch and other biblical books carefully. They concluded that the Hebrew Bible was a literary progression made up of a variety of layers of material that were written by different authors and later assembled and edited.[14]

Other modern scholars, basing their conclusions on recent archaeological discoveries in the Middle East, have specifically contradicted many biblical stories, even the story of the Exodus itself.[15] Although many Jews are not troubled by these new developments, others are profoundly disturbed. The most traditional groups among the Jewish people continue to believe literally in the Bible as the eternal word of God and dismiss modern research as a passing fad. More liberal Jews claim that the literal accuracy of biblical stories does not affect the sound morality and ethics of biblical law, which remains valid. They claim that myth and legend constitute an important component of the Jewish story and can be as meaningful as historical fact. Still a third group shrugs off these new discoveries. They are unshaken in their loyalty to Judaism, the Jewish people, and its history and are not concerned with the details of what they consider biblical legend.

The Changing Principles of Faith

A belief in the historical truth of the Hebrew Bible is not the only aspect of Judaism that has been questioned in the twentieth and twenty-first centuries. The very definition and existence of God is being questioned.

During biblical times, faith in God—or in the gods—was taken for granted, and this faith continued well into the eighteenth century. People who denied faith in God, or even expressed doubts, were considered pariahs and were shunned by society. But gradually, opinions softened and both Jews and non-Jews became more tolerant of unbelievers.

Accordingly, belief in God and in the nature of God has changed. The Bible described God in many different ways: as "a jealous God," "a just God," and "a merciful God" who cared about people. God was described with masculine pronouns and imagined in anthropomorphic terms. In Exodus, God has "a strong hand and an outstretched arm." God appears in a black cloud or in a burning bush and His presence is tangible and real.

Although some of these images continue today, most believing Jews accept Maimonides's more sophisticated view of God: God is one, meaning a single unified power; God is incorporeal, having no body or concrete form; and God is eternal.[16] This definition is the essence of Maimonides's 13 principles of faith.

Beyond those principles, there is no clear agreement by Jews on the meaning of God or whether God clearly intervenes in the affairs of humans. Jewish views run the gamut from a strictly literal, biblical faith, to doubts about the very existence of God. Some Jews posit the idea that God can be found in humanity's inclination to do good, or that God is simply the power of nature that orders and controls the universe but not the people in it. Others say God exists within the community of Israel, meaning that wherever a group of Jews gathers to pray, God is present.

Faith is not a prerequisite for Jews, however. It is viewed as a gift that not everyone is privileged to enjoy. For Jews, the important thing is not belief but behavior. Whatever a person believes, he or she must follow the commandments and behave as though there is a God.

Belief in an Afterlife

If the nature of God has no definitive answer in Judaism, the questions of life after death, heaven and hell, and the definition of the soul are perhaps even more unclear. And these concepts, too, have undergone many changes in Jewish thought from biblical times to the present.

Although the Bible does mention *Sheol*, a kind of shadowy afterlife (Numbers 16:33)[17] and relates that the prophet Elijah was transported "heavenward" in a fiery chariot (II Kings 2:11), the early biblical texts never describe heaven or explain the concept of life after death. In later texts that relate to the period of the Second Temple, when many Jews died a martyr's death, the concept of immortality and resurrection to heaven became more dominant.

These ideas were further developed during Talmudic times when the sages spoke of the Olam haBa ("The World to Come"), a purely spiritual realm lit by the Divine Presence of God. The Talmud also explicitly confirmed the idea of the immortality of the soul. As with all Talmudic texts, however, the sages' opinions were divided concerning the afterlife and a consensus is difficult to find. In general, the rabbis all seemed to agree that the soul continues after death. The righteous souls return to Paradise, referred to in the Hebrew texts as *gan eden*, the "Garden of Eden," while the wicked go to *Giehinnom*. Giehinnom, the rough equivalent of Hell, is never fully described but it is understood that this is only a temporary place. When the Messiah comes there will be a general redemption and no more need of Giehinnom.

The Concept of the Messiah

There are some biblical allusions to the Messiah, but the idea of Messiah is mainly postbiblical and came as a reaction to political and military losses. The original belief, however, did not claim that the Messiah would be a supernatural being. The Messiah (a Hebrew word that means "the anointed one") was to be human, a descendant of the great King David, who would bring the scattered children of Israel back to their land. The reign of the Messiah would usher in a political and worldly utopia and at the end of the messianic age, all righteous souls would enjoy The World to Come.

Although Judaism never conceded that the Messiah could be anything but human, their concept of the Messiah and of messianic times was certainly influenced by Christian beliefs, especially during the Middle Ages, and took on a more supernatural tone. A popular book of the period, *The Book of Zerubbabel*, described the stages leading to the end of days. The end of days meant the end of society as people knew it and the beginning of a perfect time when the world would be at peace and the principles of Judaism would rule. *The Book of Zerubbabel* also described the coming of the Messiah in great detail.

All sorts of methods were developed to enable Jews to figure out when the end of days would occur and how the Messiah would be recognized. Such speculation was a continuing aspect of medieval Judaism, and even though Maimonides warned against it, speculation continued into early modern times, often coinciding with specific persecutions of Jews.

By the late nineteenth and twentieth centuries, faith in a Messiah had been transformed once again. Theologians and philosophers of the less traditional Jewish denominations claimed that the Messiah was symbolic of a time when the world would enjoy peace under the rule of God, or when individuals would find inner peace guided by God or God's principles. The Orthodox, the most traditional of modern Jews, although differing among themselves as to exact details, still accept the idea that the Messiah will come from the line of King David. At the end of days, he will return to rule in Jerusalem and will preside over the rebuilding of the Holy Temple.

Sin and Repentance

The idea of sin can be traced throughout the Hebrew Bible and is associated mostly with the worship of other gods. The earliest of these sins occurred in the desert while the children of Israel waited for Moses to bring down the Ten Commandments. When the wait seemed too long, they became worried and built a golden calf, a representative of the Canaanite god Baal (Exodus 32:1–6). It was only through Moses's intervention that God's anger was stayed. The Israelites repented and ultimately accepted God's law. This theme—straying after other gods, punishment or threatened punishment by God, and finally, repentance and return—appears and reappears throughout biblical literature.

Individuals and groups of individuals also commit sins. When the people of Sodom sinned, God rained fire and brimstone down on them and destroyed the entire city (Genesis 19). Korah sinned by rebelling against Moses and his punishment was immediate. God opened the earth and he and his followers were swallowed up (Numbers 16).

At other times, individuals and groups repented and were saved from God's punishment. The prophet Jonah, although reluctant, was sent by God to warn the people of Nineveh to change their ways. They did and God saved the city. Later, many of Israel's judges and kings committed sins but repented and avoided God's wrath.

These stories became the paradigms for sin and repentance in Judaism. After the Babylonian exile, it was assumed that God had punished the people because of their sins. It was understood that when they became pure once again and followed God's law in its entirety, God would bring them back to the land of Israel and reinstate a Jewish king from the line of David. (The Messiah was always referred to as ben David, "the son of David.")

The Evil Inclination

The rabbis of the Talmud discussed sin frequently and believed that every human being had an evil inclination, called in Hebrew *yetzer hara*, as well as a good inclination, *yetzer hatov*. They agreed that the evil inclination was necessary in this world but that people must fight against it. The best antidote against evil was, of course, study of Torah.

There are many categories of sin. The worst sins are murder, idolatry, adultery, and incest. The sages agreed that a person should accept death rather than commit those sins. Lighter sins are less serious and are divided into two parts: sins against God and sins against humanity. For sins against God, in other words, ritual or religious offenses, repentance, and prayer are sufficient for forgiveness. For sins against humanity, the sinner must correct the wrong before being forgiven.

Israel as a Chosen People

Many people have heard the claim that Israel is the chosen people. It is mentioned in a variety of contexts throughout the Hebrew Bible. First, God chose Abraham, then he chose the 12 tribes of Israel. "Chosen" in this context means that God elected Israel to accept and to follow the Law, implying not merely privilege, but also extra obligations that cannot be ignored. God says of Abraham: "for I have singled him out ... to keep the way of the Lord by doing what is just and right" (Genesis 18:19).

The chosen relationship, first between Abraham and God and then between the nation of Israel and God, brings with it rewards in the form of special love. But because it is a covenant or agreement between God and the nation of Israel, considered binding on both sides, it is also a burden and a responsibility, with punishment for noncompliance.

Some of the Talmudic sages saw Israel as the guardian of God's law, and it was clear to them that being chosen was a privilege. The Siddur (prayer book) also expresses that idea. Several prayers include the lines: "You have chosen us from among all peoples; you have loved us and taken pleasure in us."[18]

The idea that Israel had God's special love was an important part of Jewish theology in the Middle Ages, when Jews were being persecuted throughout much of Europe and the Middle East. After the Enlightenment, however, Jews felt less comfortable with that concept and tried to redefine it. Moses Mendelssohn, a German-Jewish philosopher of the late eighteenth century (see Chapter 6), explained Israel's chosen status as a mission to pass on the special message of God to the other peoples of the world. This concept has caused much controversy among Jews and much resentment from non-Jews who understand it as an assertion of superiority.

By the twentieth century, the Reform and Reconstructionist denominations of Judaism had omitted the lines "You have chosen us" from their prayer books. The more traditional denominations have retained them, but have explained and interpreted them differently. Some Jews, however, continue to feel uncomfortable with the idea.

As with many of the other tenets of Judaism, there is disagreement. Jewish philosophers and theologians are still struggling to bring the biblical concept of a chosen people in line with Judaism's ideals of humanism and universal inclusion.

The Centrality of Israel

Part of what is considered God's special relationship to Israel has its source in a promise to Abraham. This promise, found in chapter 12 of Genesis, begins with a special mandate. "Go forth from your native land and from your father's house to the land that I will show you" (Genesis 12:1). When Abraham arrives in what was then called Canaan, God says, "I will give this land to your offspring" (Genesis 12:7).

After the descendants of the 12 tribes of Israel returned from Egypt, it was to this "promised" land that they returned. And when Israel was exiled to Babylonia, it was again this land that they longed for. One of the Psalms relates that when their Babylonian captors asked the Jewish exiles to sing a song, they answered, "How can we sing a song to the Lord on alien soil?" The Psalm continued with a pledge that has come down through the ages: "If I forget thee O Jerusalem/Let my right hand wither"(Psalms 137:4–5).

Longing for Zion (another name for Jerusalem, the city that became a symbol of the land of Israel) became a hallmark of the Jewish people throughout their exile, not only in Babylonia, but everywhere the Jews settled. In the daily and Sabbath prayers, Jews still ask God to "lead us in joy to our land and to settle our people within its borders."[19] Judah haLevi, an acclaimed Spanish-Hebrew poet of the twelfth century wrote: "My heart is in the East and I am at the edge of the West."[20] Some Jews actually did journey to their "Holy Land" during the early Middle Ages, in spite of the risks of the journey and the difficulties and dangers of living there. Immigration increased in the sixteenth and seventeenth centuries under Turkish rule.

Although an interest in returning to Zion was always an important part of Judaism, Zionism, the name given to the modern movement, was not actually organized until the 1800s. Political Zionism developed as part of a trend toward nationalism throughout Europe and was spurred on by renewed antisemitism. It was this Zionist Movement that laid the groundwork for the modern state of Israel and that focused the perpetual longing for a homeland on one united effort. Although some Jews reject Judaism's connection to one particular land, and believe that the Jews have become a universal people, they are in a distinct minority. Today, most American

Jewish Americans show their support for Israel in the annual Israel Day Parade in New York City. Here school children march carrying both American and Israeli flags. Courtesy of the author.

Jews, even though they may never actually live in Israel, consider it to be the Jewish homeland and the center for Jews everywhere. They see it especially as a refuge for Jews who are endangered in other lands and give Israel not only moral support but financial aid as well.

All Israel Is Responsible One to Another: Giving Charity

Acts of charity are considered a positive commandment for Jews, and this is reflected in the Hebrew language itself. Charity, or *tzedakah,* comes from the root word *tzedek,* or "justice," and tzedakah actually means "righteousness." The rabbis of the Talmud chose that word to emphasize the significance of charity, and it remains an important aspect of Judaism today. In fact, some modern Jews perform few of the 613 commandments, but they do observe the commandment to give money to the needy by donating large amounts to Jewish and non-Jewish charities.

The importance of helping the poor can be found throughout the Bible. The prophet Isaiah proclaimed: "this is the fast that I desire... . It is to share your bread with the hungry, And to take the wretched poor into your home; When you see the naked, to clothe him" (Isaiah 58:6–7). Giving 10 percent of one's income to the poor was considered an acceptable minimum, and charity is further encouraged by the Talmudic precept: "All Israel is responsible one for another" (Shabuot 39a). In the context of this passage, the reference to responsibility suggests that all Israelites are responsible for each other's sins. It later became broader, and Rashi interpreted it to mean that all Jews are responsible for helping each other.

In the Middle Ages, even the smallest Jewish communities had an organization to dispense charity to needy Jews, as well as to Jewish travelers who found themselves in need. Later, specific groups were founded, such as societies to bury the dead, to provide dowries for poor brides, or to feed widows and orphans. And of course, there was always a fund to support Jews living in the "land of Israel."[21]

Maimonides wrote about charity very specifically, explaining the eight forms of giving. The most virtuous form of charity is not to give alms but to lend poor persons money or to employ them or otherwise give them an opportunity for independence. The next best is to give in such a way that neither the donor nor the recipient knows the identity of the other. Less virtuous is when the donor knows the recipient but the recipient does not know the donor. If both know the identity of the other, that is less desirable. The least worthy of the eight forms of charity is to give after being asked, but reluctantly.[22]

With these standards in mind, a large number of contemporary Jewish organizations have set up funds that collect and dispense money as needed to specific causes. Most of the time, the giver and the receiver are unknown. A large percentage of Jewish donations go to support programs in Israel. In addition, in the United States, the United Jewish Appeal/Jewish Federation, B'nai Brith and its Anti-Defamation League, The American Jewish Congress, and The American Jewish Committee are just a few of hundreds of organizations that support both Jewish and non-Jewish institutions and programs in the United States.

NOTES

1. See Exodus 23:19; 34:26; Deuteronomy 14:21.

2. This ruling was extrapolated from the language in this verse (Leviticus 17:13), which deals with the generality of killing and eating birds.

3. Genesis 32:33, after describing Jacob's struggle with the angel, explains: "Therefore the children of Israel eat not the sinew of the thigh vein, which is upon the hollow of the thigh, unto this day."

4. This principle is cited four times in the Talmud: Nederim 28a, Gittin 10b, Baba Kama 113a, and Baba Batra 54b-55a.

5. Tradition attributes this statement to Rav (Master) Simlai, a Babylonian-born scholar who lived in the land of Israel during the second half of the third century C.E. but allusions to the number 613 can be found even earlier.

6. Many Jewish scholars have enumerated this list of commandments. For the version offered by Maimonides, see *The Encyclopaedia Judaica*, 1st ed. s.v. "Commandments," cols. 763–782. This gives both the positive and negative commandments, organized according to topics, with the appropriate biblical source for each.

7. Although "non-obligatory" does not seem to bar women from practicing these commandments, in practice it did exclude women from most of them. The exception was in the case of learning Torah. If a man had no sons, then for him to follow the positive command to teach the Torah to one's children, a man had to teach his daughter. See Emily Taitz, Sondra Henry and Cheryl Tallan, *The JPS Guide to Jewish Women: 600 B.C.E.–1900 C.E.* (Philadelphia: Jewish Publication Society, 2003), p. 28.

8. This precept is discussed in many different places in the Talmud. See especially Yoma 85a and Hullin 10a in the Babylonian Talmud.

9. *Pirkei Avot* (The Sayings of the Fathers) 5:24. Pirkei Avot was included in the original Mishnah but is different in format and content and is often read separately.

10. Ezra Shereshevsky, *Rashi: The Man and His World* (New York: Sepher-Hermon Press, 1982).

11. Isadore Twersky, *A Maimonides Reader* (New York: Behrman House, 1972), pp. 16–19.

12. See *Encyclopaedia Judaica*, 1st ed., s.v. "Jacob ben Asher." The complete quote is "reasoning had become faulty, controversy had increased, opinions had multiplied, so that there is no *halakhic* ruling which is free from differences of opinion."

13. Ismar Elbogen, *Jewish Liturgy: A Comprehensive History*, trans. by Raymond P. Scheindlein (Philadelphia: Jewish Publication Society, 1993). See especially pp. 187–218.

14. Julius Wellhausen, *Prolegomena to the History of Israel* (New York: Meridian Books, 1957) is the major proponent of this theory.

15. Israel Finkelstein and Neil Asher Silberman, *The Bible Unearthed: Archeology's New Vision of Ancient Israel and the Origin of Its Sacred Texts* (Atlanta: Free Press, 2001). The findings of these archaeologists remain controversial and there are certainly archaeological data pointing to the existence of Hebrews in the desert. Clearly, the evidence is incomplete.

16. Twersky, *A Maimonides Reader,* pp. 14, 20.

17. *Sheol* is first mentioned in Numbers 16:33, in the story of Korah who was swallowed by the earth as a punishment for challenging Moses's leadership. The quote is: "They went down alive into Sheol, with all that belonged to them; the earth closed over them and they vanished from the midst of the congregation." Other mentions of *Sheol* can be found in Psalms 6:6 and Isaiah 38:18.

18. These lines are part of the *Amidah* prayer, the *Alenu* prayer, and also the blessing over the wine on Sabbath.

19. This is part of the *Amidah* prayer, recited daily and on Sabbaths. This translation is from *Siddur Sim Shalom* (New York: United Synagogue of America, 1985), 435.

20. T. Carmi, *The Penguin Book of Hebrew Verse* (New York: Penguin Press, 1981), 347.

21. The land that in ancient times belonged to the people of Israel was given many different names over the centuries. Under the Romans, it was called Judea and, later became part of Syria. Still, later it was named Palestine and today it is the modern state of Israel. To avoid confusion, that particular area of land will be referred to throughout this volume in nonpolitical terms as *the Land of Israel,* meaning the geographical area that comprised, first, the united land of the ancient Israelites and then the two divisions of Israel and Judah.

22. Maimonides's eight ways of giving tzedakah are outlined in his *Mishneh Torah,* "Yad Mattanot Anniyim" 10:7–12.

3

BRANCHES

Judaism is a culture that, from its earliest history, allowed for a variety of opinions. Differing schools of thought can be traced back to the beginnings of Judaism. Throughout the centuries, new ideas, interpretations, and practices have continued to develop. Although most people today are aware of Orthodox, Conservative, and Reform Judaism, there are (and have been) many other branches. Some have made profound impressions on Jewish life, whereas others appealed to a small minority. Each branch has its own emphasis, and adherents believe in a specific philosophy or set of practices, but all branches are included under the umbrella of Judaism.

Because early Judaism always allowed for dissent, and left room for both majority and minority opinions, it was relatively simple for different branches to develop. The first evidence of such branches is found in ancient Israel, with the separation of the kingdom into two separate states. In succeeding centuries, differing Jewish points of view have been represented by separate political spheres and separate schools of legal/religious thought.

EARLY DIVISIONS

Sadducees, Pharisees, and Essenes

Two of the earliest divisions to appear among the people of ancient Israel were the Sadducees and the Pharisees. They represented two different interests that became fully developed during the Hasmonean era (164–63 B.C.E.) when the Maccabees became kings in the land of Israel (then called

Judea). The Sadducees and the Pharisees might be considered political parties; the Sadducees were the party of the ruling classes, the High Priests and the rich; the Pharisees were the party of the sages and the common people. In addition, both had very specific ideas about how to interpret Jewish law.

Because the rulers of the Hasmonean dynasty served both as kings and High Priests in the Temple, and there were no elections, the Sadducees never truly lost power. However, the Pharisees were the overwhelming majority in the land, and their influence with the people served as a balance.[1]

A third group that surfaced during those years was the Essenes, representing a very small minority of the Israelites. The Essenes were close to the Pharisees in their beliefs but were more extreme in their religious practices. They were scrupulous in their attention to laws of purity and denounced worldly goods and political power. The Essenes were mostly farmers and herdsmen who shared a communal house and attempted to live a holy life. Some say they denounced marriage. Many historians believe that the Essene philosophy was an important influence on Jesus.[2]

Even after the reign of the Hasmoneans, these three branches continued. They represented similar interests during King Herod's time (ca. 37 B.C.E.) but were overshadowed by other factions under Roman rule. The new political groups differed in regard to how or whether to rebel against Rome. Their disagreement was so bitter that they actually fought each other at the same time as they fought the Roman army, contributing to the destruction of Jerusalem.[3] These divisions did not totally disappear until after the final defeat of the Jewish nation by the Romans in 135 C.E.

The Houses of Hillel and Shammai

With the end of the institution of the Temple and its priesthood, and with no Jewish leader strong enough to successfully challenge the rule of Rome, political/national interests became much less relevant. But other divisions, those that concentrated mainly on different ideas about Jewish law, developed new importance.

The houses of Hillel and Shammai were the best known of the emerging schools of thought toward the end of the Second Temple period. They were named for two sages who lived at an earlier time and represented two different ways of interpreting the law. Hillel, the more liberal of the two men, was a patriarch (spiritual leader) in the land of Israel beginning in approximately 10 B.C.E. and was extremely influential among the scholars.

He believed in interpreting the laws of the Bible as much as possible so that they would easily apply to changing times. Shammai, also a great scholar, was the more rigid of the two. He believed that biblical law should remain as intact as possible.

After the deaths of both these sages, the Pharisees divided into two groups: those who followed the house of Shammai and those who followed the house of Hillel. The Mishnah, the first written interpretation of biblical law (often called the oral law), indicated that the majority opinion was almost always with Hillel. But Shammai and his followers were an important and respected minority.

The houses of Hillel and Shammai had some violent disagreements, but they always respected each other and their opinions were recognized equally as "the words of the living God" (Eruvin, 13b). Both Hillel and Shammai always remained loyal to the law, and neither tried to separate from the main body of Judaism or to deny the validity of the Talmud in the way that the Karaites later did.

Karaism

The word "Karaism" (pronounced kara-ism), comes from the Hebrew root word *kara* meaning "text or reading." It is assumed to refer to the Karaite's insistence on keeping the original Jewish text, the Bible, as unchanged as possible. Karaism, the first and only branch of Judaism to actively rebel against the accepted conclusions of the rabbis, developed at the end of the eighth century, beginning with Anan ben (son of) David.[4]

Anan ben David was a Jewish scholar from an important and respected family in Babylonia. He thought that the interpretations of the law, as they appeared in the Mishnah and the Talmud, were unacceptable; instead he drew his own conclusions from biblical law.

Those legal interpretations might have simply developed into another school, just as the methods and opinions of Shammai and Hillel had. But Anan himself insisted that those who believed in his conclusions had to withdraw from those who did not. He wrote: "father or mother, brothers or children who do not serve heaven in our fashion are persons from whom we are duty bound to separate."[5]

From that time, the Karaites became an autonomous group. Other Karaite leaders arose after Anan ben David, but they never tried to repair the breach between themselves and the rabbis and gaonim, the scholars who headed the academies in Babylonia (see also Chapter 1). Karaite rules be-

came stricter and much closer to the biblical text. The Karaite leaders saw
their form of Judaism as a continuation of the tradition of the Sadducees,
who had also believed in limiting the interpretation of biblical law.[6] Although the Karaites did develop a range of opinions, they remained firmly
in opposition to the Talmud and to the authority of the sages and leaders,
whose goal was to unify Jewish practices and traditions.

The Karaites were at their strongest during the tenth and eleventh centuries. At first, they were centered in Jerusalem and throughout the Middle
East. They later moved north, into Byzantium (present-day Turkey) and
areas around the Black Sea. Although they were strongly opposed by the
mainstream rabbinic Jews, they were nevertheless always regarded as Jews
and almost always included with the Jews in any governmental decrees or
anti-Jewish laws.[7]

Until recently, Karaites continued living autonomously and remained a
separate group. In 1932, before World War II, there were 10,000 Karaites in
Russia, most in the Crimea, and another 2,500 outside of Russia.[8] Karaites
still exist today, some in Israel and some in the United States, but most have
now cast their lot with mainstream Judaism.

GEOGRAPHICAL BRANCHES

Gradually, despite differing opinions and occasional rebellions against rabbinic decisions, the influence of the Talmud grew. The gaonim in Babylonia
became the authorities on questions of law, and, by the tenth century, their
teachings had spread and been accepted throughout the Jewish world. However, other changes were taking place among Jews that proved to be divisive,
too, and made unification of practice for all Jews more and more difficult.

As a Jewish homeland faded into the past, and Jews moved farther from
their original geographical base in the land of Israel, they adapted many of
the customs and languages of their host cultures. Although they continued
to practice Judaism and tried to follow the laws the rabbis had set out in the
Talmud, small changes inevitably took place in each area. In addition, most
of the Jews in these dispersed communities now spoke limited Hebrew or
none at all.

By the early Middle Ages, Jews lived in approximately five different geographical and cultural areas: the Middle East and North Africa; Spain and
Portugal; northern Europe, especially France and Germany; Italy; and Byzantium. In each of these areas, the people spoke different languages and
developed individual customs and practices.

As the Jewish population of the Diaspora grew, the Jews in major population centers set up their own academies to teach and interpret Jewish law according to their own needs and ideas. They no longer depended on the gaonim and the academies in Babylonia. As a result, more differences arose.

Jews in Arab Lands

The Jews who remained in the Middle East and North Africa came under the rule of Islam by the middle of the seventh century c.e. They began to speak Arabic instead of Hebrew or Aramaic and had to adapt to the laws of Islam concerning minorities.[9] These laws required that Jews wear a special symbol on their clothing to differentiate them from Muslims and put certain limits on their way of life. For example, their synagogues were not allowed to be taller than mosques and they had to pay special taxes that were not required of Muslims.[10]

Despite these restrictions, Jews flourished under Muslim rule and gradually began to adopt some of the ways of Islam. Many of their documents were now written in Judeo-Arabic, a new combination of Arabic and Hebrew, written in the Hebrew alphabet. Following Muslim custom, they became stricter about keeping women away from public view and away from men outside their own families.

Like Arab men, Jewish men were permitted to take more than one wife. This practice was common among Jews during biblical and post-biblical times but was less accepted under Roman rule. When it became more popular again, it led to unique clauses in Jewish marriage contracts that tried to protect brides. Many contracts stipulated that a husband was not allowed to take a second wife without the approval of his first wife. Other marriage contracts allowed the wife, as well as the husband, to initiate a divorce, a custom that was unique to Jews in Arab lands.[11] Changes in dress developed as well. Male Jews wore turbans and females wore special colored veils and sashes, marking Arabic-speaking Jews as quite different from those living in the West.

The Sephardim

Sepharad is the Hebrew word that designated the lands of the Iberian Peninsula, now Spain and Portugal. Jews had lived here as early as the second century c.e. and developed communities shortly after. By the tenth century they had their own language, called Ladino. It was similar to early Castillian Spanish but was intermixed with Hebrew words and was written in the Hebrew alphabet.

Because Spain and parts of Portugal were under Muslim rule from the early part of the eighth century, Jews living there adopted many Muslim customs. Jewish men also practiced polygyny, meaning they could marry more than one wife. Arabic as well as Spanish was spoken by much of the Jewish population, and the writings of the great Arab philosophers influenced Jewish philosophy and theology.

The Sephardi Jews prospered under Muslim rule for hundreds of years. Many worked closely with the nobility. Others became famous poets and writers, imitating the methods and forms of the great Arabic poets and grammarians. Jews ruled their own communities according to Jewish law and Jewish scholars wrote important law codes. They also developed a unique melody and style of praying.

As the Catholics gradually reconquered Spain from the Muslims, they first allowed the Jews to remain. The Catholic Church tried to convert the Jews, but few were willing to accept Christianity. Finally, the Jews were expelled from all of Spain in 1492. The Jews of Portugal met a similar fate in 1497. Those who did not leave Portugal in time were forcibly converted to Christianity, placed under the watchful eye of the Inquisition, and barred from leaving.

The hundreds of thousands of Jewish refugees who left the Iberian Peninsula at the time of these expulsions settled in many different parts of Europe, North Africa, and the Middle East. They brought their special style of Jewish culture and language with them, and it spread and influenced other Jews. The Sephardim, however, still remain a distinct group within Judaism. Although they are now a minority of the Jews in the world, some still speak Ladino. The Sephardim often maintain separate synagogues and prefer to marry within the Sephardi community.

Ashkenazim

Ashkenaz is the Hebrew word for "Germany," and the Jews who settled in that part of Europe came to be called Ashkenazim. Ashkenazi Jews do not have quite as long a history as the Sephardim and were not as numerous, but by the fifth century, there is evidence that Jews, mostly merchants and traders, were living along the rivers of France and Germany. Many had come north from Italy. Their settlements grew slowly and independent Jewish communities probably did not develop here before the ninth century.[12] It was not until 1066 or after that Jews settled in England, brought in by the French conquerors of that land.

The Ashkenazi Jews also had their own language. Similar to Jews in the other geographic areas, the Ashkenazim based their language on what was spoken around them. It was a dialect of German, mixed with some French and Hebrew words and written in the Hebrew alphabet. Originally called Judeo-German, this language came to be called Yiddish.

Because the Jews of Germany and France lived in a Christian world and not a Muslim one, they adopted some Christian practices. One of these was the practice of monogamy, meaning men were limited to only one wife at a time. The ruling on monogamy was promulgated by one of the early sages of Germany, Rabbi Gershom of Mainz, called "the light of the Exile."[13] It never applied to Jews living under Islam and was one of the major differences between European Jews and the majority of the Jewish population that lived in non-Christian lands.

Other differences also developed, especially in ritual and prayer. Ashkenazi Jews had a distinct way of pronouncing Hebrew, quite different from the Arabic-speaking or Sephardi Jews, and the melodies of prayer were closer to the style of melody in northern Europe.

Following the custom of Europeans, the Ashkenazi Jews allowed their women more freedom to move about. They could work in the community and even travel alone. Such practices were much less acceptable for Jewish women who lived in lands dominated by Islamic culture.

The Ashkenazi manner of dress was different, too. Quite early in their history, the Ashkenazi Jewish men began to wear a unique, conical hat that distinguished them from the rest of the population. In the early twelfth century, Ashkenazi men also began to cover their heads while studying or praying. This tradition later spread throughout the Jewish world and became accepted practice for every male Jew. It was not until early in the thirteenth century, long after that first ruling was passed by the Muslim Caliphs (rulers of Islamic lands), that Europe's Jews were required to wear a special patch on their clothing to mark them as non-Christians.[14]

The Jews were expelled from the lands of northern Europe in quick succession, for economic or religious reasons—sometimes a combination of the two—during the later Middle Ages. They were forced to leave England in 1290, parts of France in 1306, and several German cities later in the fourteenth century. Although some of those Jewish refugees turned West, to Spain, most crossed the Rhine River and went East, spreading into the

eastern parts of Germany and the lands beyond (now the countries of Poland, Lithuania, Austria, and the Czech Republic). They took the Yiddish
language with them and adapted it to include words from the languages
that were spoken in these new areas.

The population of Jews in Eastern Europe grew and spread, especially in
Poland, Lithuania, and the Ukraine, and their communities were strong and
active, constituting one of the main centers of world Jewry from approximately 1500 until World War II.[15] During World War II, the Nazis, the ruling Fascist party in Germany, and their allies, systematically slaughtered the
Jews. After the War, it was estimated that six million Jewish men, women,
and children—a majority, but not all, Ashkenazim—had been killed. Most
of those who survived did not want to remain in Europe. They immigrated
mainly to the new state of Israel or to the United States. Some also went to
Canada, the lands of South America, and Australia. Ashkenazi Jews today
make up a majority of world Jewry and until recently, they dominated the
cultures of Israeli and American Jewry.

Italian Jews

Italy was the first European land to receive Jews. In 63 B.C.E., after Rome
first conquered Judea, Jews were brought from the land of Israel to Rome
as slaves. Although most were soon ransomed or liberated and returned to
their homeland, a small number remained in Rome. Then, with the final destruction of Jerusalem by the Romans in 68–70 C.E., another group of Jewish captives was brought to Rome and joined those already living there.

The Italian Jewish community slowly grew and spread to other cities,
especially those along the southern coast, but little is known about the first
Jewish settlers or their practices. Only after 1348 are there reliable records
of a growing Jewish community. In that year, Jews from some German cities were expelled and began migrating south into the Italian peninsula.[16]

The Italian Renaissance had considerable effect on the Jews living in Italy.
Secular education, not only for men but for women, became more common, and both women and men taught dancing and music to young people.
Many Jews became popular dance teachers and entertainers and appeared
in elaborate productions for the Italian nobility. These practices continued
in spite of the disapproval of the more conservative German rabbis.[17]

After the mid-fourteenth century, Italy had a mixed Jewish population.
Some were Ashkenazi Jews from Germany, others were the original Italian
Jews, and still others were Romaniot Jews from the Byzantine Empire to the

The main synagogue in Rome, site of the oldest Jewish community in Europe, is still used today. Courtesy of the author.

East. Almost 150 years later, when the Sephardim were expelled from the Iberian Peninsula, thousands immigrated to Italy and added to the diverse mix of Jews already living there.

The Sephardim soon outnumbered the Italian Jews. They built their own synagogues or became the majority in already-established synagogues, continuing their own customs and rituals. The original Italian Jews did have a Judeo-Italian dialect and prayers were often translated from the original Hebrew into Italian, but today, only a few true Italian Jews still survive. Many were rounded up and killed during World War II. Most have been assimilated into the Sephardi Jewish culture.

The Jews of Byzantium

The Romaniot, the Jews of Turkey, Greece, and parts of the Balkans, experienced the same process of reverse assimilation as the Italians. These lands, once called Byzantium or the Byzantine Empire, had a sizable population of native Jews, at least from the time of Roman Emperor Constantine in the early fourth century. They spoke mostly Greek and developed some unique practices of their own.

Because Byzantium was first a Christian empire, the Jews there followed Rabbi Gershom's ruling and did not take more than one wife. But some of their marriage customs differed from those of the Ashkenazim. For example, Romaniot Jews allowed a man and woman to live together even before marriage, and women used the public baths for ritual purification rather than their own ritual bath (*mikveh*) as stipulated by Jewish law.[18]

The early Byzantine emperors issued harsh, anti-Jewish rulings, but despite a considerable amount of conversion to Christianity—much of it forced—Jewish culture remained strong. Its main influences were first, the land of Israel, where Jews maintained an active academy until the fifth century, and then the Jewish communities of southern Italy, which, until the tenth century, were part of the Byzantine Empire.

In 1204, when Christian Crusaders from the West invaded Constantinople, the Byzantine Empire fell and was divided up into separate constituencies, ruled by local leaders. From this time, not much is known of Romaniot practices and ways of life. In 1453, when the Muslim Turks conquered that area, the Jews fared better. Their communities were stronger and able to absorb the large numbers of Sephardim who began to arrive in the newly organized Ottoman Empire after 1492. The Turkish sultans welcomed these immigrants and the entire area now became a haven for Jews.

Today, only a very small number of Jews still live in Greece and Turkey. Most of the Greek Jews were killed in the Holocaust. The rest migrated to Israel after World War II. Turkey has a few small Jewish communities in the larger cities. Most of them are Sephardi Jews. Only recently have some Jews acknowledged their Romaniot background as separate and have begun searching for their roots in what was once the old Byzantine Empire.

TRADITIONAL RELIGION DIVIDES

After the expulsion of Jews, first from northwestern Europe and then from Spain, Portugal, and southern France, Sephardi and Ashkenazi Jews were no longer confined to specific geographical areas. They kept their own traditions and maintained their own synagogues and rituals, but they mixed more freely with each other throughout Europe and the Middle East, and they accepted each other's differences. Rabbis and scholars wrote elaborate law codes noting the different practices of the two groups and recognizing both as legitimate. This tolerance of differences began to change in the second half of the 1700s, with the appearance of a new movement, called Hasidism.

The Rise of *Hasidism*

The word *hasid* means "pious" and the followers of that movement were referred to as Hasidim, or "Pious Ones." Hasidism was begun by Israel ben Eliezer, a Jew from southern Poland whose Hebrew honorific, Ba-al Shem Tov ("Master of the Divine Name"), indicated that he was a mystic and worker of magic.

Israel Ba-al Shem Tov was a charismatic man who attracted many followers, from great rabbis and scholars to less educated men and women (see also Chapter 6). He urged Jews to overcome the hardships and miseries of daily life and worship God with joy. Many were drawn to his beliefs and a second generation elaborated on this philosophy.

The Hasidim developed an intricate mystical system, based partly on Kabbalah, a tradition that first appeared in southwestern Europe. Kabbalah literature included a description of the heavenly spheres and ritualistic methods to hasten the coming of the Messiah.[19]

Following in the footsteps of Israel Ba-al Shem Tov, many charismatic leaders (*rebbes*) set up courts in towns all over southern Poland and surrounded themselves with followers of their own. Some groups of followers became large enough to be considered as separate sects within Hasidism. Each was named for the town in which their *rebbe* lived, and the various groups still retain those names today, even though they now live elsewhere.

The most successful of the Hasidic groups was the Habad, or Lubavitcher Hasidim. HaBaD is an acronym for the Hebrew words *hesed* ("lovingkindness"), *binah* ("understanding") and *da'at* ("knowledge"), the principal beliefs of this branch of Hasidism. Lubavitch was the Russian town where their first sage, Rabbi Schneur Zalman (1745–1813), was most influential. His writings were studied meticulously by his followers and are still highly regarded. Schneur Zalman's descendants continued to lead Habad until the end of the twentieth century and the Lubavitch Hasidim have become the most numerous of all the Hasidic branches.

By the twentieth century, using modern communication techniques and a widespread system of outreach to Jews around the world, Habad brought large numbers of Jews back to the Jewish fold and has influenced many to

Hasidim going to pray at the Western Wall in Jerusalem. The different hats signify what group or sect they belong to. Courtesy of the author.

become more observant. Their most recent leader, Rabbi Menachem Schneerson (see also Chapter 6), was widely respected and some of his followers even insisted that he was the Messiah. After his death in 1994, many predicted that the Lubavitcher Movement would fade away, but it has remained strong and vibrant and has set up synagogues and centers around the world.

Opposition to Hasidism

The Hasidic Movement, with its emphasis on mysticism and spiritual experiences, and its insistence on joy in worship, stood in direct contrast to the intellectual emphasis of the majority of Jews in Eastern Europe in the 1700s. As this new and popular movement spread, a bitter controversy developed between the Hasidim and those who opposed them (the *Mitnagdim*). By 1772, leaders from each group were denouncing the other and burning each other's literature. In 1781, several rabbis issued a decree insisting that the Hasidim "must leave their communities with their wives and children ... and they should not be given a night's lodging."[20]

This virulent opposition lasted for about 30 years. By then, Hasidism had become firmly rooted in Eastern Europe, and the movement began to place more emphasis on study and less on magic. In addition, new threats to Judaism, common to both groups, were emerging: the Enlightenment and Jewish Emancipation.

The Struggle between Rationalism and Spiritualism

The Enlightenment Movement (*Haskalah* in Hebrew) began in the more industrialized lands of Western Europe by the early 1700s. It was not a Jewish movement, but rather a humanist philosophy. It stressed rationalism for everyone, and thus many Jews and Christians saw it as a direct attack on spiritualism in general and religion in particular.

Enlightenment ideas often went along with emancipation for Jews. In the more economically prosperous countries, governments were granting the Jews equal rights. This trend was hastened by the French Revolution that began in 1789, and the subsequent conquest of Europe by Napoleon throughout the early 1800s.

Slowly, Enlightenment and Emancipation movements spread eastward, into the less industrialized parts of Europe. They took hold first in Germany and Austria and then in Eastern Europe, where the majority of European Jews now lived, and appealed to large numbers. The modern emphasis on rationalism made many Jews think that their religion was old-fashioned and mired in superstition. Moreover, some enlightened Christians suggested that if Jews embraced the Enlightenment's philosophy of rational thought and gave up their outdated religion, they could enter the modern world as equals. In countries where Jews had long suffered from intolerance and were just beginning to enjoy equal rights and new opportunities, these ideas were appealing. The philosophy of the Enlightenment even led some Jews to convert to what was considered the more "rational" religion of Christianity.

In an effort to counter the effects that the Enlightenment was having on individual Jews, Jewish leaders attempted to improve their own culture and update their beliefs, demonstrating that Judaism was also a rational and moral religion.

Moses Mendelssohn (1729–1786), a respected Jewish scholar from Berlin, was among the first to insist that a Jew could follow Jewish law and still function in the modern world (see also Chapter 6). Others followed his example, organizing to improve Jewish education and to modernize Jewish ritual. One of the first and most successful of these attempts began in Germany in the first decade of the1800s.

The Beginning of Reform Judaism

At first, the attempt to reform Jewish ritual and prayer concentrated simply on style. The traditional religious service dated back to an earlier time and did not conform to modern ideas of beauty and spirituality. Some Jews thought that Jewish ritual could become more meaningful if they shortened the prayers, added a choir and an organ, and established a more dignified atmosphere in the synagogue. When these changes were successful on a private basis, the Hamburg Temple was established in 1818 and followed those new standards.

Many rabbis saw such innovations as meaningful, explaining that they were following in the footsteps of all the Jewish sages of the past who had sought to make Jewish law relevant to changing times. They did not want to break away from Judaism or form a new sect. What they wanted was a new look for Judaism. One of the principal spokesmen for these new ideas was Abraham Geiger (1810–1874), a German Jew from Frankfurt. Geiger became a rabbi and was one of the leaders of the early Reform Movement.[21]

Opposition to the Reform Movement was quick to develop among the more traditional Jews, and this opposition grew as the founders of the new movement made increasingly radical changes. One of the most shocking of the new ideas was that Jews were no longer a nation but a religious community. Following this philosophy, they removed any mention of a return to Zion (another name for Jerusalem and thus a synonym for the land of Israel) from the traditional prayer book.

Succeeding generations of reformers claimed that a large proportion of Jewish law—laws of purity, the rules referring to forbidden foods, and the rituals reflecting practice in the ancient Temple in Jerusalem—were written for a time long past. They simply no longer applied to modern Jews. Reformers also translated most of the prayer book into German, claiming that Jews no longer understood Hebrew, and allowed men and women to sit together rather than in separate sections of the synagogue. These new standards were relevant and meaningful to many, especially the more secularly educated and emancipated Jews.

Reform Judaism spread from Germany into Hungary and England and then across the sea to North America, where it made its greatest inroads. In the United States, one of the earliest and most outspoken leaders of the Reform Movement was Rabbi Isaac Meyer Wise. He is given credit for its early growth and for establishing its major institutions, the Union of

American Hebrew Congregations, Hebrew Union College, and the Central Conference of American Rabbis.[22]

The first official philosophy of Reform Judaism was proclaimed in the Pittsburgh Platform of 1885. This statement of purpose reasserted the radical ideas that had caused strong opposition among the Jews in Germany. Reform leaders in Pittsburgh insisted that the most important parts of Judaism were not ritual but rather moral and ethical. They also denied a continuing tie to the land of Israel and asserted that Jews were loyal and devoted citizens of the United States.

Barely half a century later, in 1937, the Columbus Platform changed Reform philosophy again and Reform leaders reclaimed the idea of Zion as a homeland for the Jewish people. Every Jew, they now realized, had an obligation to help further the establishment of a Jewish state, not only as a haven for persecuted Jews but also as the center of Jewish culture. At the same time, Reform Jews acknowledged that holidays, Sabbaths, and other rituals were important for Judaism. Members of Reform Temples were encouraged to return to tradition.

Throughout its almost 200-year history of change, the Reform Movement has held fast to one ancient Jewish understanding. The Torah must be interpreted and reinterpreted to maintain it as a meaningful document, relevant to the needs of the Jewish people.

The Reform Movement is active in England (where it is called Liberal Judaism), and there are a few Reform congregations in Western Europe (especially in France, Germany, and Hungary) and in the state of Israel. But Reform synagogues are most numerous in the United States. They continue to evolve while turning more and more to tradition and ritual, albeit with a modern spin, emphasizing community standards but stressing individual conscience most of all.

Reform Judaism is a fast-growing and forward-looking movement that becomes ever more relevant as Jews evolve and change.

Orthodox Judaism

Contrary to popular assumptions, Orthodox Judaism as it is known today is not the same Judaism that existed before European emancipation of Jews. In its own way, it is also revolutionary and, like Reform Judaism, first gathered strength as a reaction to the Enlightenment. Later, it reacted against the Reform Movement specifically.

From the beginning of the nineteenth century, the goal of most Jewish leaders and rabbis was to stop the defection of Jews away from Judaism. With the opening of the Jewish ghettos and the emancipation of individual Jews in the evolving nation states of Europe, it was becoming possible, for the first time, for Jews to live outside the Jewish community. They could accomplish this either through conversion to Christianity or simply by living a secular life, something that was not really possible before the eighteenth century. While the new Reform Movement claimed that making Jewish life easier and more modern could halt the trend away from Judaism, the traditionalists saw these kinds of reforms as an imitation of Christianity and a step toward total assimilation. They searched for another way.

One of the early leaders of the Orthodox Movement was Rabbi Samson ben Rafael Hirsch (1808–1888), a German Jew born in Hamburg who later worked in Frankfurt. Hirsch's father, Rafael, was an active opponent of the new Reform synagogue in Hamburg, and Samson took a similar position. Although he was not against certain changes to the service—in fact, during his younger years, he had been a friend of Abraham Geiger—he strongly objected to any rejection of Jewish law and to any questioning of the principles of Jewish faith. It was not Judaism that was in need of reform, insisted Hirsch, but Jews.

One of Rabbi Samson Hirsch's first books was called *Nineteen Letters on Judaism.* This work, written in the form of letters between two young Jews, laid out his ideas on Jewish education and contained many innovations. Although many Jewish communities, especially those in central and Eastern Europe, concentrated only on study of the Talmud, Hirsch believed in the study of the Bible as well. He also encouraged young Jews to get a university education so they could function successfully in the secular world. But he was not ready to compromise on the study or the observance of Judaism.

"Torah with *derekh eretz* was Hirsch's watchword. *Derekh eretz* means, literally "the way of the land"; and this quote, originally found in *The Sayings of the Fathers* (*Pirkei Avot* 2:2), the last book of the Mishnah, implied that a person should be educated in Torah (that is, Jewish law) and also in secular studies. Jews could study in university and be enlightened citizens and still maintain loyalty to the laws of Judaism. Hirsch and his followers refused to accept the Reformists' idea that biblical law was developed over time to meet the needs of society. God gave the Torah in one revelation, they believed, and therefore individuals were not free to choose which laws to follow.

Although other factions among the traditionalists disagreed with various aspects of Hirsch's philosophy, they did agree on two main points: the God-given nature of the Torah and the laws, and the authority of the rabbis who interpreted those laws. They rejected the new concept of a science of Judaism, explaining that observance of all the 613 commandments must come before speculation, before the objective study of those commandments.[23]

Eventually, Reform and Orthodox split and formed two separate branches of Judaism. Encouraged by the Orthodox faction, the two groups agreed that if a Jew wanted to leave the congregation because of differences of religious principle, that Jew could do so without leaving Judaism. This ruling was passed in Hungary in 1868 and in Germany in 1876. From that time on, synagogues were labeled either Reform or Orthodox.[24]

Orthodox Judaism was sometimes referred to as neo-Orthodoxy to emphasize its differences from the earlier mainstream traditionalists. It spread West from Germany into France and England and was brought into the United States by German immigrants. It also spread eastward, capturing the imaginations of many of the more enlightened traditionalists of Eastern Europe. The Hasidim did not join forces with neo-Orthodoxy. They remain separate, maintaining their own organizations and leaders and their own schools.

Similar to the Reform Movement, Orthodoxy has also tended to become more traditional with time. By the end of the twentieth century, Orthodox Judaism was moving toward stricter positions on observance and becoming less tolerant of Jews who held more relaxed ideas concerning Jewish law. Their philosophy of "Torah true" Judaism has enjoyed considerable acceptance both in the United States and in Europe. In Israel, it is the only form of Judaism that is considered valid and enjoys the support of the government. In the last few decades, many young people have turned to Orthodoxy, finding in its observant way of life an answer to the ethical and moral conflicts of the modern world, and a successful guide in raising a Jewish family.

Conservative Judaism

Conservative Judaism was also conceived in Germany and was an attempt to find a middle way between the extremes of Reform and Orthodox. Originally called Historical Judaism, this philosophy stressed the progressive interpretation of Jewish law throughout the ages but insisted on retaining all of the law. This idea contrasted with the Reform view that certain laws were no longer relevant and could be ignored.

One of the men who first formed the historical school was Zacharias Frankel (1801–1875). Frankel was born in Prague but served in German cities for most of his rabbinical career. He believed that reform was needed in Judaism, but he wanted only reforms that did not conflict with the spirit of Historical Judaism. He also argued for continued use of the Hebrew language in the prayer book, and for retaining a belief in the Messiah and a hope for a return to Zion.

Frankel organized a rabbinical seminary in Breslau in 1854, where he set out the foundations of Historical Judaism. His theories quickly met with opposition from both Samson ben Rafael Hirsch and the growing Orthodox Movement, and also from Abraham Geiger, the principal Reform leader.

Although he never succeeded in establishing a strong movement in Germany, Frankel did set the standard for modern rabbinical training, and created a model that was adopted by an active group of American Jews in the late 1800s. It was in the United States that Historical Judaism became Conservative Judaism, stressing the idea of *conserving* Jewish law while updating its relevance.

The Conservative Movement in the United States developed as a reaction to Reform, which was dominant during the 1880s. The German Jew Isaac Leeser (1806–1868), an American rabbi, educator, and writer, was its first proponent, but others soon joined him, including Sabaato Morais, an Italian Jew from England, Benjamin Szold (the father of Henrietta Szold) of Hungary and Baltimore, and Cyrus Adler, then a young student at Johns Hopkins University. Most of these men had been educated in Germany, and all were traditionalists who advocated some change. Together, they organized a rabbinical seminary in 1887 to train American rabbis. The goal of The Jewish Theological Seminary, located in New York City, was "the preservation in America of the knowledge and practice of historical Judaism as ordained in the law of Moses expounded by the prophets and sages in Israel in biblical and talmudic writings."[25] In 1902, the founders invited a scholar from Cambridge University in England to head their new seminary and he accepted. His name was Solomon Schechter.

Under the leadership of Schechter, The Jewish Theological Seminary became the center of the growing Conservative Movement. Their philosophy of "tradition and change" was especially attractive to the large numbers of Eastern European Jews who were coming to the United States in the late 1880s.[26] These immigrants were looking for a traditional synagogue that also made allowances for modern life. They felt comfortable in the new Conservative congregations that were springing up in New York, Philadelphia, and some of the other cities of the eastern United States. In these synagogues, the men could read the prayers in the familiar Hebrew, but they were able to sit together with their wives and children and hear a sermon in English.

It was a good compromise for many Jews, and from the 1940s to the 1950s, the Conservative Movement was the fastest growing in the United States. By the 1970s and 1980s, however, this was changing. As the generations born in Europe began to die out, their grandchildren had less attachment to the double commitment of tradition and change. Many drifted into Reform congregations or became unaffiliated, while those who were attached to tradition saw Orthodoxy as the more authentic Judaism and joined Orthodox congregations.

Conservative Jews still believe that their philosophy has much to recommend it, but others predict a merge of Reform and Conservative. In the beginning of the twenty-first century, however, Conservative Judaism remains an important and vital movement among American Jews.

The Branches Divide

The Reform, Orthodox, and Conservative Movements were, fundamentally, divisions of Ashkenazi Jewry. Some Sephardi and Middle Eastern Jews in America did join those synagogues, especially if a Sephardi synagogue was not available. Most, however, remained in their own synagogues, more or less united, with a relaxed form of traditional Jewish practice, while the predominantly Ashkenazi congregations in the United States divided into smaller subgroups. Each subgroup exemplified new changes in ideology and each represented the interests of a small segment of the Jewish population.

Zionists and Anti-Zionists

One of the earliest ideological differences among twentieth-century Jews concerned a commitment to Zionism, the concept of a Jewish homeland in Israel. The earliest Reform platform, promulgated in 1885, had rejected Zionism, but the second platform reaffirmed loyalty to the idea of a Jewish homeland. This reversal was rejected in turn by some reformers. As political Zionism became more and more vibrant, and increasing numbers of Jews began moving there or supporting the settlers with money, a movement against it developed in the United States, especially among Reform Jews. They believed that Judaism was a religion of universal values and not a nationality. Although they did not object to individual Jews moving to Israel and settling there, they did not believe it should be considered a Jewish homeland. They were very much against what they called the preoccupation of American Jews with the Israel-Zionist ideal, insisting that American Jews should have allegiance to only one nation, the United States. In 1942, a small group of Reform rabbis established The American Council for Judaism to present their values and beliefs to the American public and to try to change the opinions of other Jews.

Although the actual establishment of the state of Israel and its military successes eventually eclipsed the American Council for Judaism, the ideas of the Council left a bitter legacy. The lingering question of Jews' dual loyalty has still not completely disappeared from American life.[27]

Orthodoxy and Its Variations

A joke that is familiar to Jews all over the world says: "Two Jews, three synagogues." This is an allusion to the Jewish tendency to disagree on philosophical issues and on matters of Jewish law, and it can be traced back to Hillel and Shammai (discussed before). Such a tendency is nowhere more apparent than among the Orthodox, because they are the group that is most concerned with Jewish law and its proper interpretation.

From the late 1800s, when the new Orthodoxy was established, there were already built-in divisions. The Hasidim remained staunchly separate and were themselves subdivided into smaller groups, each with slightly different customs and practices and different rabbinical leaders.

The original neo-Orthodox group also subdivided according to their Zionist ideals. At first, most traditional Jews believed that a Jewish state would be established only when the Messiah came. Any efforts to hasten it, they insisted, were against the will of God. But a minority, both in Europe and the United States, did believe in working for a Jewish homeland. They called themselves the Mizrahi ("Eastern") party and joined the Zionist Movement early. Today Mizrahi is one of the political parties in Israel and is supported by many Orthodox Jews there. There are still small groups, however—some actually living in Israel—who still await the Messiah and oppose the Jewish state.

Besides the issues surrounding Zionism, other minor differences developed among traditionalist Jews. These differences resulted in new subgroups, each espousing a different theory of teaching, or practice, or interpretation of the law. Some were stricter and some more lenient. Those who were the most exacting are sometimes referred to as ultra-Orthodox and they themselves are divided into different groups.

Despite these differences, however, all consider themselves proponents of "Torah-true Judaism" and recognize the authority of the ancient sages as it is interpreted by their own rabbis and leaders.

Reconstructionism

Although it began as a set of beliefs within the Conservative Movement, Reconstructionism has become a fourth branch of Judaism. It was first advanced by Mordecai Menachem Kaplan (1881–1983), a rabbi and teacher at the Conservative Jewish Theological Seminary. Kaplan taught that Judaism is a civilization that until now had been united by a belief in salvation after death. Since most Jews no longer believe that, he said, Jews must transform Judaism into a civilization where salvation can be found in *this* world. This kind of salvation can be reached through self-improvement and working toward a just society. Ritual, Kaplan believed, was not law. Rather it was a means to Jewish survival and personal spiritual growth. The choice of which rituals to follow was not up to rabbinic authority but to the individual Jew.[28]

Kaplan gained many adherents among the faculty and students at the Seminary and, by 1922, had formed a group in New York City called The Society for the Advancement of Judaism. This society functioned as a synagogue and as a place where Kaplan and his followers could meet and develop and discuss their ideas. It is still in existence today.

Originally, there was no intention of creating a separate movement, and Kaplan continued teaching at the Seminary until 1963, when he was 82 years old. His Reconstructionist Prayer Book for the Sabbath was published in 1945. In 1968, a separate Reconstructionist Rabbinical Seminary was established in Philadelphia, and, by 1970, there were 10 congregations affiliated with the Federation of Reconstructionist Congregations and Fellowships. Reconstructionism remains the smallest of all the denominations but its influence has been felt throughout the Reform and Conservative Movements.

A Variety of Different Opinions and Groups

By the last few decades of the twentieth century, modern life in North America, Europe, and Israel had greatly affected Jewish life and created many new divisions among Jews. These divisions are as varied as the Jewish people themselves. Some stress tradition and the return to older ways; others have tried to incorporate new, secular philosophies into Judaism. Feminism is one secular philosophy that has made important inroads into Jewish religion and culture.

Feminism in Jewish Society

In the past, women had a low social status, and, in Jewish law, the work of men and women was clearly divided. A firm belief in such a "division of function" still exists among the most observant Jews today. Many of the less traditional, however, have embraced the feminist movement and applied it to Judaism. Citing the Jewish commitment to fairness and justice, they believe that women's traditional position is merely a reflection of an older social system and not the will of God.

As a result of feminism, and a commitment to equal rights for both sexes, more and more Jewish women participate freely in society, enjoying careers and full equality. They claim the right to choose whether to marry and raise a family, to find alternative sources for childcare, or to have no children.

Although Orthodox Jews consider having children a commandment that they would never avoid, even the most traditional of Jewish women see their roles changing and expanding. They often work at careers outside the home, and, increasingly they are given the opportunity to study Jewish law. Although in the less strict denominations (especially in the United States) most women have been granted equal rights in Jewish ritual, the traditional precepts and assumptions that limit women and deny their obligation in performing the commandments have remained mostly unchallenged by Orthodox women. Some Orthodox Jews suggest that woman's role is a privileged one and the absence of obligation for her suggests a spiritual superiority.[29]

Jewish Renewal Movement

Jewish Renewal is a modern movement that crosses denominational lines. True to its Jewish roots, it seeks to redefine the ancient Jewish techniques of achieving spirituality and make them relevant to today's Jews. To

This woman's prayer group is one of many organized since the 1980s. They offer Orthodox women a chance to learn and experience the rituals of communal prayer that were traditionally open only to men. This service is in celebration of Purim, and some women are wearing funny hats in the spirit of the holiday. Courtesy of Rita Gordonson.

further those ends, its most important leader, Rabbi Zalman Schechter-Shalomi, has adopted ideas, rituals, and beliefs from the Hasidic Movement and the Reconstructionist Movement, as well as Hinduism, Buddhism, and other world religions.

Jewish Renewal first appeared in the 1970s and appealed especially to young, counter-culture Jews who were rebelling against the Establishment and searching for new meaning in Judaism.[30] They sought spiritual fulfillment through retreats, healing services, and classes in meditation and Kaballah (the ancient tradition of mystical learning) and set up a variety of organizations to serve those needs. These included a retreat house and a main center, originally called B'nai Or (Children of Light) and now known as Aleph, the Alliance for Jewish Renewal. Located in Philadelphia, Aleph serves as a training center for rabbis. The movement now has a prayer book of its own and is composed of a network of approximately 50 congregations and 60 rabbis.

Jewish Renewal has been described as a "hands-on, mystically inflected, radically egalitarian, liturgically inventive, neo-Hasidic approach" to Judaism.[31] Although not widespread, Jewish Renewal has had a considerable impact on the major movements and on individual rabbis and lay Jews in North America and Israel. It has also considerably influenced the Havurah Movement in the United States.

The Havurah Movement

One of the newer branches of Judaism that has borrowed ideas from both Jewish feminism and Jewish Renewal is the Havurah Movement. The word *havurah* is Hebrew for "group of friends," and from ancient times it referred to a group of people who study together. The movement traces its beginnings to 1968 in Somerville, Massachusetts, a suburb of Boston, when a young rabbi named Arthur Green founded a single havurah. The Somerville Havurah was extremely successful, first attracting Jewish students from the local colleges and then young families and singles who were looking for a Jewish service where they could feel at home. Similar groups spread quickly, usually forming in or near a university campus but including nonstudents as well.

The aim of those first *havurot* (plural of havurah) was to create a meaningful, egalitarian service, with no rabbi or acknowledged leader. The members themselves led the services and studied together and men and women participated equally in all Jewish rituals.

Each havurah may have a different emphasis. Some are traditional and some are more liberal in choosing which rituals to follow. Many were organized just for study and members gradually began to celebrate holidays and family events together. Others began as prayer groups and expanded from there to include study and group celebrations. Some set up their own schools to teach their children about Judaism.

Since 1968 the Havurah Movement has grown considerably, and today there is a National Havurah Committee that unites the groups. Although it does not set down rules to follow or demand specific philosophies of its members, it does make learning materials available and publishes a newsletter so that problems and solutions can be shared and information exchanged. Each year the Havurah Committee holds a convention that is attended by hundreds of members throughout the United States and Canada.[32]

Other Subdivisions in Judaism

The study of Kaballah has enjoyed renewed popularity both among Jews and non-Jews. Although traditional Jewish teaching has always claimed that people need to be well educated and grounded in Jewish law before they can begin to study and understand Jewish mysticism, many Jews have ignored that warning. Small numbers of modern Jews who have felt alienated from Jewish practices and Jewish life find meaning in this esoteric method of getting close to God by the use of mystical formulas, sometimes using combinations of letters of the Hebrew alphabet. The most recent devotee of Kaballah study is the pop singer Madonna.

As long as Judaism remains a dynamic culture and religion, open to individual interpretation, Jews will probably continue to mold Jewish law and ritual to their own vision. New groups continually form and re-form, stressing one belief or another, one geographical tradition or another, or one of a variety of forms of worship. These differences often make for a lively interchange among Jews. Occasionally they lead to criticism and strife, even outright rejection. Ultimately, however, all are recognized as Jews, living under the giant and constantly expanding umbrella of Judaism.

NOTES

1. H.H. Ben-Sasson, ed., *A History of the Jewish People* (Cambridge, Mass.: Harvard University Press, 1976), Book 3, *The Period of the Second Temple* by M. Stern, pp. 235–238.

2. Ibid. pp. 272–273.

3. Ibid. pp. 300–303. Flavius Josephus, a historian of the period, reported on the war in his book *The Jewish War,* part of *The Complete Works of Josephus* (Cambridge, MA: Harvard University Press, 1925).

4. Zvi Ankori, *Karaites in Byzantium: The Formative Years, 970–1100* (New York: AMS Press, 1968), p. 6.

5. Quoted from E. Harkavy, ed., *Book of Commandments* (St. Petersburg: 1903), p. 7, as cited by Ben Sasson, *A History of the Jewish People,* p. 441.

6. Ankori, *Karaites in Byzantium,* p. 20.

7. The exception was during the nineteenth century when Karaites attempted to exempt themselves from the harsh, anti-Jewish decrees in Russia by claiming to be non-Jews. See *Encyclopaedia Judaica* (1st ed.), s.v. "Karaites: Under Russian Rule."

8. *Encyclopaedia Judaica,* s.v. "Karaites: Numbers of Karaites."

9. Aramaic, a language closely related to Hebrew, was the language of the entire Middle East by the end of the Second Temple period. Much of the Talmud (but not the Mishnah) is written in Aramaic.

10. Norman A. Stillman, *The Jews of Arab Lands: A History and Source Book* (Philadelphia: Jewish Publication Society, 1979), pp. 22–39, 157–162.

11. Mordecai A. Friedman, *Jewish Marriage in Palestine: A Cairo Geniza Study,* 2 vols. (Tel Aviv: Tel Aviv University Press, 1980).

12. Kenneth Stow, *Alienated Minority: The Jews of Medieval Latin Europe* (Cambridge, Mass.: Harvard University Press, 1992), p. 89.

13. For the full text and background of this ruling, as well as other rulings made by Rabbi Gershom, see Louis Finkelstein, *Jewish Self-Government in the Middle Ages* (New York: Philipp Feldheim, 1964), pp. 23–35.

14. Solomon Grayzel, *The Church and the Jews in the XIIIth Century,* vol. 2 (Detroit: Wayne State University Press, 1989), pp. 8; 30, n.43. The decree was issued by the Fourth Lateran Council of the Church. The earlier Muslim decree was issued in the year 850. See Stillman, *Jews of Arab Lands,* p. 167.

15. Jews came into Russia only in the late 1700s, when parts of Poland and the Ukraine were annexed to the Russian Empire. Although the Russian government tried to keep Jews from spreading into the rest of Russia, they were not completely successful. The Jews who managed to migrate East, into the areas around Moscow and St. Petersburg, escaped being victims of the Holocaust, but later, were not allowed to leave Russia.

16. Robert Bonfils, *Jewish Life in Renaissance Italy* (Berkeley: University of California Press, 1994), p. 20.

17. Don Harran, "Jewish Musical Culture: Leon de Modena" in *The Jews of Early Modern Venice,* eds. Robert C. Davis and Benjamin Ravid (Baltimore: Johns Hopkins University Press, 2001), pp. 212–213.

18. Steven Bowman, *The Jews of Byzantium: 1204–1353* (Tuscaloosa, Ala.: University of Alabama Press, 1985), p. 124.

19. Gershom Scholem, *Major Trends in Jewish Mysticism* (1941; 3rd ed. New York: Schocken Books, 1954), pp. 327–330.

20. *Encyclopaedia Judaica,* s.v. "Hasidism: Opposition to Hasidism."

21. W. Gunther Plaut, *The Rise of Reform Judaism* (New York: World Union for Progressive Judaism, 1963); *The Growth of Reform Judaism* (New York: World Union for Progressive Judaism, 1965).

22. Israel Knox, "Isaac Meyer Wise," in *Great Jewish Personalities in Modern Times,* ed. Simon Noveck (n.p., B'nai Brith Great Book Series, 1960), pp. 112–114.

23. See I. Grunfeld, ed. and trans. *Three Generations: The Influence of Samson Rafael Hirsch on Jewish Life and Thought* (1958) for a full explanation of Hirsch's philosophy.

24. For a fuller development of these events, see H.H. Ben Sasson, ed., *A History of the Jewish People:* Part 6, "The Modern Period," pp. 847–852.

25. *Encyclopaedia Judaica,* s.v. "Conservative Judaism."

26. Mordecai Waxman, ed., *Tradition and Change: The Development of Conservative Judaism* (New York: Burning Bush Press, 1958).

27. Elmer Berger, *Judaism or Jewish Nationalism: The Alternative to Zionism* (New York: Bookman Association, 1957).

28. Some of the books written by Mordecai Kaplan explaining his views include *Judaism as a Civilization* (Philadelphia: Jewish Publication Society, 1934; new ed. 1994); *The Purpose and Meaning of Jewish Existence* (Philadelphia: Jewish Publication Society, 1964), and *The Meaning of God in Modern Jewish Religion* (1937; new ed. Detroit: Wayne State University Press, 1994).

29. See Judith Hauptman, *Rereading the Rabbis: Woman's Voice* (Boulder, CO: Westview Press, 1998), pp. 222–243 for an overview of several interpretations of the absence of obligation for women, as well as her own interpretation.

30. Michael Lerner, *Jewish Renewal: A Path to Healing and Transformation* (New York: G.P. Putnam's Sons, 1994), "Prologue," pp. 1–20.

31. Debra Nussbaum Cohen, "Renewal's Struggle for Acceptance," *The Jewish Week* (April 21, 2000), p. 1.

32. www.havurah.org is the website for this organization and posts their activities.

4

PRACTICE WORLDWIDE

This chapter presents an overview of the Jewish population throughout the world, how they are divided geographically, and how they worship. Not only mainstream Jewish communities are explored, but those outside the mainstream are also introduced. Geographical and cultural differences have led to differences in the prayer book. Despite these differences, however, the Jewish worship service has kept the same basic structure and the same core group of prayers. This enables Jews to feel at home in a synagogue, no matter where they may be. A second commonality among diverse groups of Jews around the world is their common symbols, and a third is their attachment to Israel, a symbolic homeland even for those who never go there.

WORLD JEWISH POPULATION

At the threshold of the twenty-first century, the total number of Jews was 12,950,000, less than 1 percent of the world's population of 6 billion. The largest centers of Jewish life are located in Israel (5,940,200) and the United States (5,300,000). Other concentrations of Jews can be found mainly in the democratic countries of the world. Canada has 370,500 Jews. Australia and New Zealand boast small but active Jewish communities, a combined total of 106,900 as of 2003. And a surprisingly large number of Jews make their homes in Europe.

European Demographics

Despite the Holocaust, which killed 6 million European Jews, plus the immigrations that resulted before and after World War II, and the recent rebirth of antisemitism in Europe, a sizeable Jewish population still exists on that continent.

France has the largest Jewish community in Europe, numbering close to 500,000, but most are recent Jewish immigrants from North Africa. England has a Jewish population of 300,000 and Germany ranks third with 108,000. A large majority of Jews now living in Germany have come from Russia since the 1980s.

Almost every other European nation has a small Jewish presence, sometimes not more than 100, as is the case of Slovenia and Macedonia. Even in Poland, where so many Jews were murdered in concentration camps during World War II, there is now a Jewish community of just over 3,000.[1]

Russian Jewry

Until the 1970s, the U.S.S.R. had the largest concentration of Jews in Europe. Because of the Communist ban against all religions and also because of continued antisemitism in that country, few felt free to practice their religion, and Jewish culture in all its forms was repressed. Many Russian Jews wanted to immigrate to Israel or the United States, but under the Communist regime, the Jews (along with all other Russian citizens) were not allowed to leave the country.

After a concerted effort on the part of world Jewry and pressure from American Jews and the U.S. government, the U.S.S.R granted some Jews permission to leave if they could prove that they wanted to be united with family members. From that time, and continuing after the fall of the Communist regime, Jews poured out of Russia to the freedom of Israel, the United States, and Canada. Large numbers also settled in Germany, Austria, and Italy.

Today, the Jewish population of the area that once was the Soviet Union is still sizeable but has diminished considerably, down from an original estimate of close to 3 million in the 1970s, to 389,700.[2] More than half of these Jews live in the new Russian Republic and a sizeable number (95,000) live in Ukraine.

Jewish Populations in the United States

Today, Jews living in the United States represent the most numerous and diverse population of Diaspora Jews (that is, those living outside Israel). By far the largest proportion of them, more than 2 million, are centered in the New York Metropolitan area. The next largest community is Los Angeles, California, where there are 668,000, followed by southeast Florida (498,000). Most major U.S. and Canadian cities have Jewish populations of varying sizes, and individual Jews can often be found in the most out-of-the-way places in the country. Even traditional Jews, who require the support of a Jewish community and its institutions to live a fully observant life, have found their way into the smaller towns of America, although they usually settle near a large city.

The number of Orthodox Jews who live in the United States is growing, and, as of 2002, there were 1,501 Orthodox congregations throughout this country; 352 are modern Orthodox, 346 are affiliated with Habad (Lubavitcher), and the rest identify with other Orthodox groups.[3]

Sephardi synagogues, 4 percent of the total, are almost all nominally Orthodox, although many practice a more relaxed form of Judaism than the Ashkenazi Orthodox; Conservative and Reform Jews number slightly less. In all, 26 percent of all synagogues (976 congregations) in the United States identify as Reform and 23 percent (865 congregations) are Conservative. Reconstructionist Jews have the fewest: only 99 synagogues throughout the country, representing 3 percent of the total number. Other non-Orthodox denominations have even fewer than 1 percent each. Taken together, however, these more liberal and less observant forms of Judaism are the majority, making up more than 50 percent of the synagogues and congregations (those who pray together in a place other than a synagogue).

The United States is the only nation in the world where most Jews are not Orthodox or traditional and where large numbers are not affiliated with any Jewish community even though they are free to do so.

Other Jewish Communities

Although more than 95 percent of world Jewry is concentrated in the 15 largest Jewish communities, there are Jews living in almost every corner of the known world.[4] Some are relative newcomers, having come for business purposes or as representatives of their own governments, but many have lived in these far-flung places for centuries. There are small pockets of indigenous Jews in Yemen and Libya. A handful of Jews still remain in Afghanistan, Uzbekistan, and Iran.

Other Jews have been settled in their adopted countries for less time. The Jews of South Africa and Zimbabwe (the former Rhodesia) first came to that area in the nineteenth century and helped build the country. In the 1970s and 1980s, many immigrated to Australia, North America, and Israel because they were against the Apartheid policies of the government. Today the Jewish population there numbers only 76,600.

The Caribbean Islands, Thailand, and Japan also have small Jewish communities, made up partly of older residents and converts, and partly of newcomers who have settled there for a variety of reasons. Most of these communities have synagogues and Jewish centers.

More recently, Jews live in equatorial Africa, in the Himalayas, in the northernmost cities of Alaska, and the southernmost tip of South America. Although some of these Jews have chosen not to practice Judaism, many have organized small congregations and built synagogues. They may also connect to Judaism through contact with an Israeli embassy. Their active Jewish life, especially their attachment to their Jewish identity and to the Jewish state of Israel, are two major factors that unite most Jews, no matter where they live and what language they speak. There are, however, several exceptions to a unified world Jewry.

JEWS OUTSIDE THE MAINSTREAM

Some Jews have been isolated from the rest of the Jewish world and are considered outside the mainstream. Because of that isolation, their practices and customs may be so different that other Jews refuse to acknowledge that they are Jews. This was the case concerning the Jews of Ethiopia.

Ethiopian Jews

Jews have a long history in Ethiopia, a country in eastern Africa that is near Yemen and Saudi Arabia. The Ethiopian Jews themselves claim ancestry from the son of King Solomon and the Queen of Sheba, said to have been an Ethiopian. While this has never been proved, it is clear that Jews have lived in this land from before the time of Jesus and before the Mishnah was completed in 200 C.E. Although long known as Falashas, sometimes simply as black Jews, they call themselves *Beta Israel,* which means "house of Israel."[5]

Ethiopia was a predominantly Christian country and was never conquered by the Muslims, but the Jews were not the only minority. There were—and continue to be—many ethnic groups in that area. However, during their long history, the Jews often fought against the government. When they were finally defeated in the seventeenth century, they lost the right to own land and were forced to become artisans. The Ethiopians looked down on such trades, and, from that time, the Beta Israel lost considerable status and often suffered severe discrimination and occasionally, forced conversions.

Because all Ethiopia was isolated, the Beta Israel knew nothing of the existence of other Jewish communities for many centuries. They believed they were the only Jews in the world and continued the ancient practices as they were explained in the Bible, a book that they read in their own language, Amharic. They followed biblical laws concerning the Sabbath, ritual purity, and food restrictions and observed only the holidays mentioned in the Bible (see also Chapter 5). The practice of animal sacrifice for the forgiveness of sin, as described in the book of Leviticus, was continued among the Beta Israel. They considered Jerusalem to be a holy city and believed they would all return there after the coming of the Messiah.

The Beta Israel were visited over the centuries by both Jews and non-Jews, and they gradually learned of the existence of an extensive Jewish

Kess Mola in front of his synagogue, Teda, Ethiopia, 1988. Photo by Peggy Myers.

community outside their own land. After 1948, when a Jewish State was established, a few Jews from Israel and the West came to teach them the ways of modern Judaism. Although a small number of Ethiopian Jews did migrate to Israel, until recently, most stayed in the towns where they had lived for 2,000 years. Then in 1974, in the wake of an Ethiopian revolution, coupled with a severe famine and devastating economic hardships, the Beta Israel left their homes and crossed the borders into neighboring lands. They asked for asylum in Israel, their ancient homeland.

The rabbis in Israel questioned whether the Beta Israel were really Jews and whether they were qualified to come to Israel under the Law of Return, which allowed any Jew to return to the homeland for any reason. For many years the question was debated while the Ethiopian Jews languished in refugee camps. Some were smuggled out individually or as family groups and brought to Israel or to other countries.

Finally, in 1984, after intense pressure from Jews outside Ethiopia, especially American Jews who were also sensitive to the racial issues involved, Israel agreed to accept the Beta Israel. In a major airlift, called "Operation Moses," 8,000 Ethiopian Jews were flown to Israel where the government began the long process of their settlement and absorption. A smaller number came after them in "Operation Joshua." But relatives of those already in Israel still remain in Ethiopia, waiting for permission to join their families and communities. Many of those left behind had previously converted to Christianity, and their status is still under review by the Chief Rabbinate.

The Jews of China and India

Unlike Ethiopia, a country that is geographically close to the Middle East and to the land of Israel, China and India are far away. And yet, Jews found their way there. About 500 Jews journeyed East from Iraq to China in approximately 1100 C.E. They came by caravan, along the Silk Road, well traveled by merchants and foreign traders from the West, and settled in the city of Kaifeng. These Middle Eastern Jews were welcomed by the Chinese and lived comfortably in that city for many generations, gradually intermarrying with the local population but retaining their separate identity as Jews. According to an old tradition, the Emperor, who was unable to pronounce their Hebrew names, gave them Chinese surnames unique to them. The Chinese Jews forgot their original names over the centuries but have retained those Chinese names to this day. That is one way that they know they are Jewish.[6]

Over the centuries, many different Christian missionaries traveled to China and attempted to convert both the Chinese and the Jews. The Jews consistently resisted conversion and continued their own traditions, although their numbers dwindled. When the Communists came to power in China, all religion was suppressed, but the handful of families that were still Jewish did not completely forget their heritage.

Today, a few are seeking a return to Judaism. Xu Xin of Nanking University has been a leader in this effort. He translated the *Encyclopaedia Judaica* and several other books into Chinese and organized a Jewish Studies department at his university. In 2004, Jin Wen Jing became the first Chinese Jew to be converted back to Judaism in Israel. She is hoping that more will follow.[7]

Indian Jews are much more numerous than Chinese Jews. They settled in India early, perhaps before the destruction of the Second Temple, and historians confirm an established community there by the twelfth century. Called the *Bene Israel* (children of Israel), they lived in villages and towns throughout India and observed most of the major Jewish rituals and holidays.

During the sixteenth century, more Jews came to India for purposes of trade. Most of these were from Iraq and were more prosperous than the earlier Bene Israel. They settled mostly in Cochin, Calcutta, and Bombay.

In 1949, shortly after the establishment of the state of Israel, many Indian Jews left India for Israel. Here, they faced problems similar to those of the Ethiopians; the government of Israel refused to recognize them as authentic Jews. Considering this a serious insult, the Bene Israel held a sit-down strike in Jerusalem that lasted from 1962 to 1964, refusing to leave until their status as Jews was acknowledged. The government and the rabbis finally gave in, and from the mid-1960s there was a large influx of Indian Jews into Israel. By 1970, the population of Bene Israel Jews in the Jewish State was about 23,000; there were still 15,000 more remaining in India, with the largest community (10,000) in Bombay.[8]

More recently, another group of Indian Jews, the *B'nai Menasseh,* has surfaced. Living on the border of India and Myanmar, they claim ancestry from the ancient tribe of Menasseh, one of the ten supposedly lost tribes (see also Chapter 1). So far, the Chief Rabbis and government of Israel have not recognized them as Jews and have required that they convert. Some 700 B'nai Menasseh have done so and are presently living in the occupied territories on the West Bank. In 2005, the chief rabbis of Israel agreed to convert the rest of the B'nai Menasseh and allow them all to settle in Israel.

The Crypto-Jews of Spain and Portugal

Spain and Portugal were far less isolated from mainstream Judaism than those in the Far East, and yet the Jews living there were also cut off. Spain expelled the Jews in 1492 and most did leave. Some, however, pretended to convert so that they would be allowed to stay; but secretly they remained Jews, practicing what they could behind closed doors. If they were discovered observing any of the Jewish traditions, they were tortured and killed by the Inquisition. The Inquisition was a religious court, an arm of the Catholic Church that worked to ensure that Catholicism remained pure and free of outside influences.

In Portugal, the situation for Jews was even more difficult. The Portuguese king signed an order of expulsion in 1497, but he quickly changed his mind and forced all the Jews to convert. Thousands of Jews were trapped in Portugal for centuries. Many were caught practicing Jewish rituals and were burned to death. Others managed to escape the flames of the Inquisition and remain secretly Jewish, but they still had to pretend to be Catholics. They could not avoid being baptized, attending Church, and observing all the Christian holidays.

Over the centuries, they forgot most of the Jewish traditions and prayers. There were no Jewish calendars, no Jewish books, and no Jewish scholars to advise them. Still, they persevered, celebrating what they remembered, observing the Sabbath secretly and following the holidays described in the Bible, the only Jewish book they were allowed to own.

When Portugal became a democratic nation in the mid-1970s, Jews were once again free to practice Judaism. But they still remained fearful. When other, mainstream Jews began coming into Portugal and setting up synagogues, they looked at the Portuguese crypto-Jews as a group apart and did not welcome them. They had all been baptized, many had married Christians and raised Christian children, and they knew nothing about modern Jewish practices.

In 1992, a full 500 years after the original order of expulsion from Spain, the Spanish government rescinded that decree. The Portuguese president did the same in 1997 and officially apologized for the suffering inflicted on the Jews of Portugal for so many centuries. He admitted that he himself had some Jewish ancestry and that approximately 60 percent of the Portuguese people did as well.

At the beginning of the twenty-first century, more and more Portuguese Jews are coming forward, not only those who remained in Portugal, but also those whose ancestors had immigrated to other countries. Crypto-Jews from Brazil, Mexico, New Mexico, Cuba, and many other places in Central and South America have begun to discover their Portuguese roots and to remember the Jewish rituals practiced by parents and grandparents. But are they Jews?

Few can prove a continuous Jewish line from 1497, but many feel a spiritual tie to Judaism. They want to officially convert and unite with Jews all over the world. Other crypto-Jews insist that, in spite of continued persecution, they have always been Jews and do not need to convert.

Several Jewish organizations in Israel and the Diaspora have been working with the crypto-Jews, trying to help them return to mainstream Judaism. This issue will only be solved with time.

The Abayudaya and Lemba Jews of Africa

The Jews living in southern Africa have an even more tenuous tie to the Jewish world than the Portuguese crypto-Jews. The Lemba people trace their ancestry back to a group of Yemenite Jews who crossed into Africa. One group stayed in Ethiopia and became the Beta Israel, they believe, and the other turned South and became the Lemba tribe.

The Lemba follow many of the rituals of mainstream Jews. They circumcise their sons, slaughter animals according to ritual, do not mix milk and meat, and keep many of the laws concerning forbidden foods. Most recently, anthropologists, using DNA samples, have proven that there is a genetic link between the Lemba and other Jews.

Encouraged by these findings and urged on by their desire to connect with their origins, the Lemba have approached the South African Jewish community, asking for recognition as Jews. Knowing that many of the Lemba have practiced Christianity for many generations, the Chief Rabbi of South Africa has hesitated to do so. He claims it is a matter for world Jewry and has referred them to the Chief Rabbis in Israel.

One of the leaders of the Lemba, Matshaya Mathiva, is not deterred, however. The Lemba Jews have begun building their own synagogue near the border of Zimbabwe. Says Mathiva: "Whether we are accepted or not, Israel is our ancestral home and the Jewish people are our brothers."[9]

The Abayudaya of Uganda are Jews who do not claim descent from an ancient Jewish tribe. Their original leader, Semei Kakungulu, became a believing Jew on his own. At first, Kakungulu left Christianity only as a rebellion against the white rulers of his land, but he later came to believe sincerely in the Bible and to reject the New Testament. In 1919, he declared that he was a Jew and circumcised himself and his sons. Others followed him, but they knew nothing of Judaism except what they read in the Bible.

In 1926, Kakungulu met a Jew from the Middle East who taught him and his followers the basic beliefs and practices of Judaism and all the blessings. Several other Jews who came to Uganda continued this informal education, and today the Abayudaya consider themselves sincere and believing Jews.[10]

At the beginning of the twenty-first century, some supporters of this group brought a Conservative rabbi from the United States who officially converted the Abayudaya to Judaism. Although the Chief Rabbinate in Israel will not recognize a Conservative conversion, the Abayudaya believe that they are legitimate Jews. As of now, they do not want to move to Israel. They have two synagogues in Uganda and a Jewish primary school where the children learn Hebrew and Jewish law. The community raises some money by selling Jewish artifacts and a Jewish CD of Abayudaya-Jewish songs.

Other Groups Beyond the Mainstream

Several other groups maintain some connection to Judaism, among them the Black Hebrews who have come from the United States to settle in Israel, the Sefwi Wiawso Jews of Ghana, and a small group of Japanese who claim to be one of the ten lost tribes.[11] Another group, living near the Amazon River in Peru, South America, is descended from Jewish men who married local women in and around the city of Iquitos. Although they were heavily influenced by Catholic missionaries who came to that area, many maintained a Jewish identity. Today some of these Jewish *mestizos* (people of mixed American Indian and Spanish origin) have found their way to Israel and are attempting to reclaim Judaism for themselves.[12] As communication improves and Jews come in contact with even the most isolated places, they may find even more groups of Jews or descendants of Jews who are anxious to share Jewish heritage, culture, and religion.

WORSHIP SERVICES IN SYNAGOGUES

Differences among Jews—different denominations, languages, customs, a stress on differing aspects of Jewish law—have encouraged the reorganization and rewriting of the standard siddur, the Jewish prayer book, and its translation into many languages.

Prayer Book Variations

Today, there are even more daily and Sabbath prayer books than there are branches of Judaism. Some are only in Hebrew, some offer Hebrew side by side with the language of the area, and some have hardly any Hebrew in them. Jewish scholars representing many different schools of thought have edited and reedited the traditional version. Reform and Reconstructionist editors have shortened the siddur considerably and kept Hebrew to a minimum, whereas Conservative Jews have tried to maintain much of the original. Their emphasis has been to create more modern and meaningful translations.

Orthodox and other traditional groups have kept most, if not all, of the inherited prayers, some dating back to gaonic times or earlier. Hasidic Jews always used a different prayer book than regular Orthodox congregations and continue to do so. Their siddur derives from the one used by the famed mystic, Rabbi Isaac Luria, who lived in the land of Israel during the sixteenth century.

Many new translations of the standard prayer book have been offered over the centuries, with readings added as well as eliminated. And yet, there are enough commonalties to enable Jews to feel at home and find their way in a synagogue service, no matter where they may be.

The Three Parts of the Prayer Service

Almost every Jewish service, whether for Sabbath or for a holiday, is divided into three sections, originally structured according to the order of sacrifice in the ancient Temple. The first section, the *Shaharit* (Morning Service), begins with all the blessings a devout Jew is obligated to recite each morning. It also includes the Sh'ma prayer, claiming that "God is One." This means God is a unique Being whose unity cannot be divided into different aspects. The Sh'ma is the credo for all believing Jews everywhere and most services, no matter how innovative or different, cannot eliminate this single line: "Hear O Israel, the Lord our God is One" (Deuteronomy 6:4), which a Jew is obligated to say twice a day.[13] Even in synagogues where the Hebrew language is not used for prayer, the Sh'ma will likely be recited in Hebrew.

Another basic element of the Morning Service is the *Amidah.* This means, literally "the standing." It is the silent prayer that includes 18 set benedictions—although they are different for Sabbath than for the other days—and is recited while standing. While the Amidah has undergone many changes over the centuries, and the more liberal Jewish denominations may shorten it considerably, it remains an important centerpiece of Jewish prayer.

Finally, the morning service ends with the *Kaddish* prayer. Kaddish is essentially a prayer blessing God. It is in Aramaic rather than Hebrew and contains the lines: "May His great name be blessed forever," and "Blessed be the name of His majestic glory forever." These lines were considered consolations, and so the prayer was also adopted for use as a memorial prayer for the dead. It is recited at the end of the Morning Prayer and on Sabbaths and holidays, at the end of each subsequent section.

On days when the Torah is read (Mondays, Thursdays, Saturdays, and all Jewish holidays), the second part of the service begins with ceremonies and blessings recited when the Torah scroll is taken from its ark. Then the people who are being honored are each called up to recite a blessing. This honor is referred to as an *aliyah,* meaning "going up," because the individual goes up to a raised platform from where the Torah is read.

The person receiving the aliyah may read a small section of the Torah or simply recite the blessings while an official reader reads from the scroll in Hebrew. These blessings, usually, but not always, in the Hebrew language, are chanted or recited both before and after the reading. Until recently, this honor was afforded only to Jewish men. By the second half of the twentieth century, the Reform Movement began allowing women to be called to the Torah, and shortly after, a Conservative Movement ruling did the same. It took a long time, however, for those rabbinical decisions to become accepted in individual congregations, and some still may not allow women to participate in this way.

A reading of a section from the *Haftarah,* the books of the Prophets, usually follows the reading of the biblical passages, with different blessings before and after this reading as well. The Torah service ends with special ceremonies and then the scroll is returned to the ark. If there is a sermon, it is usually offered after the Torah is replaced.

The third part of the service, called *Musaf* (meaning "additional"), is added to Sabbath and holiday services. Musaf repeats most of the Shaharit service, with the exception of the morning prayers. It includes the Sh'ma, the Amidah, and a special Kaddish prayer for mourners, and it usually closes with a hymn.

Additional material, such as poetry or appropriate passages from the Torah and various other biblical books, are added for Sabbaths and for particular holidays or events. Most prayer books include a prayer for the leader of the individual country where the congregation is located, as well as a prayer for the Jewish leaders and for the state of Israel and those who defend and live in it.

Regular Torah Readings

In every congregation, the five books of the Torah are read from beginning to end during the course of the year. This yearly cycle begins two weeks after the New Year, usually in late September or early October (see also Chapter 5) and continues until the year is over. Then it begins again. For each passage in the Torah, there is a corresponding passage from the

A Portion of the Torah is read in the synagogue three times a week. Scrolls of the Torah are kept in an ark at the front of the synagogue and are adorned with beautiful covers. Courtesy of the author.

Haftarah, the Prophets. In fact, many Jewish calendars indicate the passage to be read each Sabbath. On Mondays and Thursdays, part of the same Torah reading is repeated during the course of weekday services.

Those who read from the Torah or Haftarah usually sing the words according to a special kind of note system, creating a chant that is often particularly identified with Jewish prayer. The Arabic-speaking Jews, the Sephardim, and the Ashkenazim have their own systems of notes, and so the rendition of the Torah reading may sound quite different in different synagogues. Many liberal congregations do not chant the Torah at all, and some read it only in English. But the order of the readings and the text of the blessings are always the same everywhere.

Recently, some synagogues have made the decision to read the Torah in a triannual rather than an annual cycle. This had been done in the past and means that each portion is shorter and the cycle of readings takes three years to complete instead of one. The triannial cycle shortens the prayer service considerably, because the Torah reading is only one-third the length. The blessings and ceremonies surrounding the Torah service, however, do not change.

Dressing for Prayer

One thing that male Jews all over the world have in common is that they wrap themselves in a prayer shawl, called, in Hebrew, a *tallit* (or *tallis* in the Ashkenazi pronunciation) when they pray. A tallit is a rectangular garment, often with blue or other colored stripes, with fringes on the four corners. It is draped over the shoulders on weekday, Sabbath, and holiday services (although not at Friday evening prayers). This reflects a direct command-ment from the Bible in which God speaks to Moses, saying: "Speak to the Israelite people and instruct them to make for themselves fringes (*tsitsit*) on the corners of their garments throughout the generations. Let them at-tach a cord of blue-violet to the fringe at each corner. This shall be your fringe" (Numbers 15:37–41).

The tallit is familiar to all Jews, even those who belong to the most liberal of Reform congregations that do not require them. There is a special bless-ing to recite when putting on a tallit, and it must be handled respectfully, as a religious object.

Among Orthodox groups who follow the letter of the law, boys and men wear the prescribed fringes at all time in the form of a *tallit katan* (small tallit) that fits underneath their clothing. This is in addition to the tallit

The Tallit (prayer shawl) was once used only by men. Today, women in the more liberal branches of Judaism are beginning to wear them, acknowledging the commandment to wear fringes as a reminder of God's law. Courtesy of Vivian Krasnov.

worn just for services. It serves as a constant reminder that the commandments should not be limited to times of prayer.

Since the 1970s in the United States and Canada, many women—pointing out that the commandment to wear fringes was addressed to all of Israel, women as well as men—have begun wearing *tallitot* (plural of tallit), too. Although first regarded as strange, as if women were wearing men's clothing, it has become more and more accepted in Reform, Conservative, and Reconstructionist synagogues in North America.

The traditional head covering is even more widely known than the tallit and is considered by some to be the hallmark of the Jewish man. The custom for men to cover their heads when studying Jewish texts, during prayer, or when reciting a blessing, was intended to show deference and respect to God and developed slowly over the centuries. By the twelfth century, it was universally adopted by Jewish scholars living in western Germany and gradually spread from there throughout the Jewish world. Usually this head covering is a small cap, called a *kippah* in Hebrew, and a *yarmulke* in Yiddish.

In Orthodox and Conservative congregations, married women are also expected to wear hats during prayer or when entering a synagogue. This custom, however, does not originate from the belief that covering the head shows respect to God. It is a manifestation of the idea that women must be modest.

In ancient times, in the Middle East, modesty was a social norm for all women. They were expected, even commanded to veil themselves and not flaunt their beauty in front of men. This custom took different forms among different cultures. Muslims demanded that women completely cover their bodies, heads, and faces; Christians expected women to cover their hair only. Among Jews, the tradition of modesty focused on married women. A woman covered her hair after marriage to indicate that she must no longer be attractive to any man except her husband.

Over the centuries, the demand for women to be modest became stricter, and in some communities in Eastern Europe women were expected to shave their hair off after marriage and cover their heads with a scarf or hat. This was in line with the idea of "putting a fence around the Torah" (see also Chapter 2). Because there was no Jewish law stipulating what kind of head covering to use, women in Renaissance Italy, imitating the practice of the French nobility, began covering their heads with elaborate wigs.[14] Although the rabbis strongly disapproved, the custom held and spread north into Germany and then eastward into Poland. Gradually, the rabbis changed their rulings and in modern times the wearing of a wig has become widely accepted among the religiously observant as a sign of modesty. But even if a woman wears a wig over her own hair, she is still expected to cover her head with a hat in the synagogue.

Conservative and Reform Jewish women consider the idea of women's modesty to be a tradition, not a commandment. However, it is a custom in Conservative and some Reconstructionist synagogues for married women to cover their heads during prayer. These head coverings may range from a small piece of lace, or an embroidered kippah, to an elaborate hat. Some *kippot* (plural of kippah) are now designed especially for women and are made from woven wire and decorative beads, although these have not yet found their way into Orthodox circles. Reform Jewish women do not follow the custom of covering the hair.

The Regularity of Prayers

Jewish law requires that a Jew pray three times each day: at sunrise (the shaharit service), once during the afternoon (the *minhah* service), and again at sunset (the *ma'ariv* service). Although most Jews no longer follow this regimen, many still do. To make it easier for those who work, the afternoon service was moved up so that it takes place just before sunset and is immediately followed by the evening prayer. While tradition only expected men to be bound by this commandment, many women have also begun to attend these daily, brief services.

The Minyan

Although praying alone, at home, is always acceptable, congregational prayer is considered more meaningful and therefore more desirable because it connects a Jew with the community. But to pray as a congregation and to include the repetition of the Amidah prayer, the Kaddish, and the chanting of the Torah and Haftarah, a minyan is required. A minyan is a quorom of 10 men older than age 13. Once 10 men are present, a full service can be conducted. Judaism does not require that a rabbi be present or that the service be held in a synagogue.

Reform Jews no longer require a minyan. The Conservative Movement has allowed women to be counted in a minyan since 1973, but the Orthodox recognize only men for a legal minyan and still separate men and women in their synagogues. The Orthodox usage may not represent the majority in the United States, but most synagogues around the world and in Israel keep to the traditional ways. Women sit in separate sections, are not called up to the Torah, and are not counted in a minyan of 10.

UNIVERSAL SYMBOLS OF JUDAISM

The Menorah

The original symbol by which the Jewish people was recognized was a menorah, a seven-branched candelabrum. It was one of the main adornments of the Holy Temple in Jerusalem and was reproduced on ancient coins and on bas-reliefs found in archaeological ruins. The top of the Arch of Titus, the triumphal arch erected in Rome to commemorate victory over the Jews, shows Roman soldiers carrying away the golden menorah from the Temple.

After the final destruction of the Temple and its artifacts, drawings and carvings of menorot (plural of menorah) appeared throughout the Diaspora, especially on tombstones, but this symbol was gradually replaced during the Middle Ages by the Star of David. Today, a giant menorah, made of stone, stands in front of the Israel Parliament (Knesset) building in Jerusalem as a reminder of the past. In modern times, however, most references

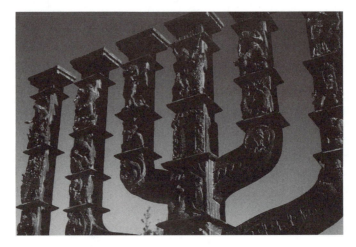

The seven-branched menorah is the most ancient symbol of Judaism. This large stone menorah stands in front of Israel's Parliament (Knesset) building in Jerusalem. Courtesy of the author.

to a menorah usually mean the nine-branched candelabrum, adapted from the original and used on Hanukkah.

The Star of David and the *Hai*

The origin of the six-pointed Star of David is unclear. Some archaeologists trace it back to prebiblical times and find evidence of it even in paganism. Others claim that it was the symbol used on King David's shield when he went into battle. And in fact, in Hebrew it is called *magen* David (the shield of David). Whatever its origins, however, it began to replace the seven-branched menorah only in the thirteenth or fourteenth centuries at the earliest, and it was still later that gravestones bore this symbol.

Today, the Star of David appears on almost every synagogue and official Jewish building. In countries where Jews are free and do not suffer persecution, individual Jews proudly wear stars of David around their necks, as jewelry and as a mark of identity.

An alternative to the Jewish star, and almost as popular among modern Jews as a piece of jewelry is the word *hai,* meaning "life." These two letters of the Hebrew alphabet, the *het* and the *yod*, have a double symbolism. The Hebrew letters themselves mark the wearer as a Jew, and the meaning of the word is an affirmation of the continued survival of the Jewish people.

Before the Arabic system of numbering was established, Hebrew speakers gave each Hebrew letter a numerical value, and these numbers are still used today in Hebrew texts. The two Hebrew letters in hai, 8 and 10, equal 18. Because of this, the number 18 has special significance for Jews. When a Jew gives a gift of money, or a charitable donation, they will often give it in multiples of 18 and refer to it as "hai," meaning $18, "double hai" ($36) or even "10 times hai" ($180).

The Mezuzah

The Bible records God's command to the Israelites concerning the law: "Take to heart these instructions with which I charge you this day. Impress them upon your children. Recite them when you stay at home and when you are away, when you lie down and when you get up ... inscribe them on the doorposts of your house and on your gates" (Deuteronomy 6:6–9).

This order to inscribe them on the doorposts (*mezuzot*) of the house is repeated again in Deuteronomy 11:13-21 and was accepted as one of God's 613 commandments. The Talmudic sages considered the mezuzah to be one of the seven precepts that were symbols of God's love for Israel (Menahot 43b). The others included *tefillin*, two small boxes containing the text of the Sh'ma prayer that a man was commanded to wear on his forehead and left arm during weekday prayers. Tefillin was counted as two precepts since there were two boxes. The remaining four precepts were the *tzitzit*, fringes that God had commanded Jews to hear on the four corners of a special garment (see also Chapter 5).

The earliest signs of the use of mezuzot are from the period of the Second Temple, and the practice has continued into the twenty-first century.[15] The mezuzah is a small holder containing a scroll of parchment. The parchment, made from the skin of a kosher animal and written by a Jewish scribe, contains the biblical command from the two verses of Deuteronomy. It is rolled up in such a way that the letters symbolizing God's name are in the center and show through the container's opening. These mezuzot are placed not only on the entrance door of the home, but also on each room (not including storerooms or bathrooms). Today, they can also be found in buildings and offices housing Jewish institutions, organizations, and synagogues, although there is no biblical precedent for this.

The mezuzah must be affixed on the upper third of the doorway, on the right side as you enter the house, slanting inward. There is a special prayer to recite when it is first put on, and the ceremony attaching a mezuzah to a new residence is called *hanukkat habayit* (the dedication of the house). When leaving or entering a house or any building that has a mezuzah, many

A Mezuzah, containing a specific text from
the Bible, is the traditional mark of a Jewish
home. This silver mezuzah case dates back
to nineteenth-century Europe. The circlets
at either end are for attaching it to the door
post. Courtesy of Temple Israel Museum,
Great Neck, New York.

traditional Jews touch it with the fingers and then kiss their fingers to show
their reverence for the word of God.

The practice of mezuzah is one of the most widespread of all Jewish ceremonial commandments, and the containers housing the scrolls have developed into a Jewish art form. Today mezuzot come in all shapes and sizes
and are made from a variety of materials, from silver and wood to other
metals, ceramics, and papier-mâché.

ATTACHMENT TO AND SUPPORT FOR ISRAEL AND
WORLD JEWRY

Scattered throughout the world for centuries, Jews have never had a
single recognized leader. In a few countries, especially in Europe and the
Middle East, Jews have Chief Rabbis who represent their own community

to the government, but they have little power to impose their view of Jewish law and still less influence on Jewish politics. There is no Jewish individual that can unite world Jewry under the banner of Judaism. Yet there is one factor that does have the power to bring most Jews together with their contemporaries throughout the world. That factor is an attachment to Israel. Although the modern state of Israel dates only from 1948, Jews have felt both a spiritual and tangible connection to that land that dates back to the beginnings of the Diaspora, even before the Common Era.

Ancient Connections to the Land of Israel

In ancient times, Jews living outside their land routinely sent a half-shekel contribution to help support the Holy Temple in Jerusalem and tried to make at least one pilgrimage to that city for a holiday celebration. After Rome's final defeat of Judea, and the destruction of the Temple in the first century of the Common Era, the Roman government insisted that Jews now pay their half-shekel to Rome.[16] This became a special tax exacted from all Jews living in the Empire and was continued in a variety of forms by succeeding governments. Although Jews bitterly resented this tax, they had no choice but to pay.

Despite the special tax on Jews, Jewish commitment to what came to be called "the Holy Land" did not diminish. There was no longer a central Temple or a Jewish government to support, but there was always a small number of Jews living in the land of Israel. Some had never left and others had returned there for religious reasons, to study and pray for the coming of the Messiah. The land itself, however, mostly abandoned, offered little if any opportunity to earn a living until the late nineteenth century, when Zionist pioneers began settling there. Until then, many of the Jews living in the land of Israel were supported by charity from Diaspora Jews.[17] Even the poorest Jews felt an obligation to give a small amount to help their brothers and sisters in the land of Israel.

Throughout the 2,000 years of exile, Jews continually prayed for the welfare of Zion and asked God to gather the exiles from the four corners of the world and return them to their own land. When the state of Israel was established, that prayer was answered. Israel opened its doors to Jewish refugees literally from the four corners of the world. Jews came from war-torn Europe, the countries of the Middle East, North Africa and Ethiopia, India, and the Americas. Most were escaping oppression or had been expelled from their own countries.

Support for Israel Today

Today, the prayer for the ingathering of the exiles is still included in many prayer books, but most Diaspora Jews who recite it do not themselves plan to settle in Israel. They are comfortable in their adopted lands and are loyal to their governments, but they still feel a responsibility to support a Jewish state. Many say it is important for Jews who need a haven from persecution, but others insist that the very existence of a Jewish state unites Jews and makes the Diaspora more secure.

Many American Jews are concerned that the policies of the United States government be favorable to Israel. To that end, a significant number of Jews in the American Jewish community support a pro-Israel lobby called the American-Israel Public Affairs Committee (AIPAC). Through outreach programs and publications, they actively try to educate government and nongovernment officials, as well as college students and the general population, about the interests of Israel and urge support of the Jewish state.

Charity for the Homeland

Long before the state of Israel was established, and before organizations were regularly channeling money into Israel, Jews had found ways to help those living in "the Holy Land." Money was collected by individual men, often rabbis, who would take a percentage for themselves and bring the rest to the scholars studying in *yeshivot* (religious academies) in the land of Israel. With the beginning of the Zionist Movement and the immigration of young pioneers committed to working the land and reviving the area, this kind of collection became less accepted. Instead, specific charities were set up like the Jewish National Fund (JNF).

The main purpose of the JNF, established in 1901 at the First Zionist Congress, was to purchase land in Israel for Jewish settlement and reclaim it for agriculture. Since then, JNF has drained swamps and planted millions of trees in Israel. Its leaders continue to fulfill a commitment to help make the desert bloom.[18]

Another major Jewish group that was formed almost exclusively to help Jews living in Israel is the United Jewish Appeal. This organization, founded in 1939, was based in the United States and was committed to collecting funds for a Jewish state and for Jewish refugees from Europe. They later joined with the Jewish Federation, an association that concentrated its energies on helping Jews in the United States and Canada. Now known everywhere as UJA-Federation, it is one of the most active charities in Israel, supporting hospitals, schools, and relief groups of every kind. UJA-Federation raises millions of dollars in North America, and its projects help not only Israeli Jews, but Israeli Arabs as well. In the United States, UJA-Federation contributes funds for the needs of both Jews and non-Jews.[19]

Zionist Organizations

Zionist associations, committed to creating a Jewish state, were first set up in Europe in the late 1800s, representing different political positions and different religious interests. They quickly established branches in North America and are still active today. They raise money for Israel, urge people to support their ideas for Israeli government policies, and encourage Jews to emigrate to Israel. Although Israel has not attracted large numbers of immigrants from the United States, some American Jews do decide to live there and there is a growing "anglo" community, especially in Jerusalem and Tel Aviv.

The first women's Zionist organization in the United States began through the efforts of one American Jewish woman from Baltimore, Henrietta Szold. On a trip to the land of Israel (then called Palestine) early in the twentieth century, Szold was struck by the lack of doctors, hospitals, and medical supplies. She returned home determined to help and, in 1912, founded Hadassah.[20]

Branches of Hadassah raised enough money to fund the first nursing school in prestate Israel. They continued raising funds and established Hadassah Hospital, still one of the best in the Middle East. Committed to helping patients of every religion and nationality, Hadassah Hospital is largely supported by money from American Jewish women.

Many other women's Zionist organizations followed Hadassah and American and Canadian women raise large amounts of money for projects in Israel and to aid World Jewry.

Secular Jews and Israel

During the nineteenth and twentieth centuries, support for Israel has been a comfortable way for nonbelieving Jews to identify with Judaism. There are many Jews who are not interested in following Jewish law in any way. They may not affiliate with a synagogue and may even question a belief

Henrietta Szold, 1938. Photograph by Ganan's
Studio. Courtesy of Hadassah, The Women's
Zionist Organization of America, Inc.

in God or declare themselves to be atheists. Yet they still feel a cultural and
ethnic connection to the Jewish people.

In the Diaspora, such a connection can be expressed in several ways.
Jews may support a particular, nonreligious Zionist organization or give
money to various Jewish charities not connected to religion. Or secular
Jews may forge a connection by working to foster Jewish culture in any of
its many forms: Jewish theater and music, Hebrew or Yiddish language and
literature, Jewish newspapers, cultural (but nonreligious) summer camps
for children, and so on.

Despite such a large variety of possibilities, many secular Jews become
estranged from Judaism and assimilate into the majority culture. This is especially easy in the West where there is a strong separation of Church and
State and non-Jews are more accepting of Jews. Today, the rate of intermarriage in the United States is at an all time high of 50 percent or more. Although some of the spouses convert to Judaism and the offspring of those

marriages will remain Jewish, many will be lost to the Jewish people. This will certainly be reflected in the Jewish population figures around the world. The most recent census acknowledges the existence of other Jews who do not identify with Judaism in any way and thus fall through the cracks and are not counted.

In Israel it is easier to be a secular Jew without losing a Jewish connection. Nonreligious or nonpracticing Jews make up a large majority of Israel's Jewish population. A recent estimate is that 14 percent of the people in Israel are Orthodox and 14 percent are Muslim or Christian Arabs. The rest are more or less secular Jews. They may go to synagogue once or twice a year or not at all. And yet, they never lose their Jewish connection.

It is easy to be Jewish in Israel, say the Israeli Jews. All the Jewish holidays are celebrated as national holidays and the shops are closed on the Jewish Sabbath. Their everyday language, Hebrew, is the ancient language of the Jewish people. They live surrounded by the archaeological remains of their ancient homeland in a cultural melting pot that offers something for everyone. Often, it is precisely this that draws Jews from the free countries of the world to Israel, a Jewish homeland where it is easy to be Jewish.

NOTES

1. All population figures are from *The American Jewish Year Book,* vol. 103 (American Jewish Committee, 2003).

2. Elie Wiesel, *The Jews of Silence*, trans. by Neal Kozodoy (New York: Signet Books, 1967), p. vii; *Encyclopaedia Judaica* (1st ed.), s.v. "Russia," gives a slightly lower number but admits that the Russian census counted only those Jews who declared their nationality as Jewish and their language as Yiddish.

3. *American Jewish Year Book,* vol. 102 (American Jewish Committee, 2002).

4. *American Jewish Year Book,* vol. 103 (American Jewish Committee, 2003), p. 610.

5. *Falasha* is a word in Amharic, the Ethiopian language. It comes from the word *melas,* "to uproot." For this and other information about Ethiopian Jews see Teshome G. Wagaw, *For Our Soul: Ethiopian Jews in Israel* (Detroit: Wayne State University Press, 1993), pp. 1–29.

6. Xu Xin with Beverly Friend, *Legends of the Chinese Jews of Kaifeng* (Hoboken, NJ: K'tav, 1995).

7. Michael Freund, "How Wen-Jing Became 'Shalva': Chinese Jewish Descendant Returns to Judaism" *Jerusalem Post* (June 22, 2004), p. 5.

8. *Encyclopaedia Judaica* (1st ed.), s.v. "India: Contemporary Period."

9. This quote is from *The Scribe: the Magazine of Babylonian Jewry* and can be found on line at http://www.dangoor.com/72page25.html (accessed May 27, 2005).

10. Jewish Virtual Library (A Division of the American-Israeli Cooperative Enterprise): http://www.jewishvirtuallibrary.org/source/Judaism/uganda1.html (accessed May 27, 2005).

11. These and many other such groups are introduced in Karen Primak, ed. *Under One Canopy:Readings in Jewish Diversity* published by Kulanu, a Jewish organization that supports nonmainstream Jewish communities.

12. Ariel Segal, *Jews of the Amazon: Self Exile in Paradise* (Philadelphia: Jewish Publication Society, 1999).

13. For this reason, the Sh'ma is recited twice a day, in the morning and evening service. The one exception is the daily minha (afternoon) service.

14. Taitz, Henry and Tallan, *The JPS Guide to Jewish Women*, p. 224.

15. *Encyclopaedia Judaica*, s.v. "Mezuzah."

16. Shmuel Safrai, "The Jews in the Land of Israel (70–335 C.E.)," in *A History of the Jewish People*, ed. by H.H. Ben Sasson (Cambridge, MA: Harvard University Press, 1976), p. 317.

17. Walter Laqueur, *A History of Zionism* (New York: Schocken Books, 1972; reprint, 1989), p. 42.

18. *Encyclopaedia Judaica*, s.v. "Jewish National Fund."

19. *Encyclopaedia Judaica*, s.v. "United Jewish Appeal."

20. Lacqueur, *History of Zionism*, p. 160.

5

RITUALS AND HOLIDAYS

This chapter outlines the rituals attached to both the life-cycle events of Jews and the holidays that occur throughout the calendar year. Ceremonies for each event and holiday are described, along with the significance of the rituals and the different variations. Holidays are divided into several categories. First are the holidays that the Bible has instructed the Jews to observe. Second are the holidays that developed after the biblical period. The last category includes holidays and commemorations concerning events that occurred in more recent times.

PAUSES AND BLESSINGS

"Jewish ritual is the *discipline of pause and focus,*" wrote Rabbi David Wolpe, a contemporary Jewish theologian.[1] This is a good way to explain any ritual. Rituals and holidays interrupt the everyday routines, force people to pause, and give them a structure that helps them focus on something special. That special something may be the celebration of a new year or an important life-cycle event, or it may be something as simple as eating a piece of bread or seeing a rainbow. In Judaism, there are special blessings to recite after being saved from danger, upon seeing a funeral, while putting on a prayer shawl (tallit), or when tasting a new food. There are blessings for the new moon and for the celebration of harvest holidays. In fact, there is a Jewish blessing for almost every occurrence, and each one begins with the same words: "Blessed are You, Lord our God, King of the Universe, who has blessed us with the commandments and commanded us to." Such simple prayers and blessings force Jews to stop their daily routines, if only for a moment, and think. They encourage Jews to be thankful for what they have, to be grateful for an end of suffering or pain, to rejoice on holidays, or to appreciate life in the face of death.

LIFE CYCLE CUSTOMS

In every religion or culture there are special rituals revolving around life-cycle events such as birth, passing from childhood to adulthood, marriage, and death. At these meaningful times, ritual becomes particularly important to Jews precisely because they help to focus on the event and give it meaning beyond everyday life.

Birth: Entering into the Covenant

Because the first commandment in the Bible is "be fruitful and multiply" (Genesis 1:28), giving birth to children has significance beyond the immediate satisfaction of creating a life. It is fulfilling the will of God. In biblical times, after giving birth a woman was obligated to offer a sacrifice in the Temple (Leviticus 12:2–6). Although Jews no longer serve God by sacrificing animals or presenting offerings of food, parents of new born children often go to the synagogue to say a blessing and perhaps to be called up to the Torah (the first five books of the Bible that are read regularly in the synagogue service). If the baby is a girl, they will announce her name at this time.

If the child is a boy, he is welcomed into the community of Israel with a more elaborate ritual involving circumcision and blessings and ceremonies for the parents, grandparents, and godparents. This event may take place either in the synagogue, at home, or in a separate hall or other space.

Circumcision involves cutting off the foreskin of the penis and is usually done in a special ceremony called a *brit milah*. The word *brit* means "covenant" and refers to the covenant Abraham made with God (Genesis 17: 10–12); *milah* means "circumcision." (Brit is often pronounced *bris* in the United States and other places where Ashkenazi Jews are dominant.)

The brit or bris usually takes place when the infant is eight days old. The procedure is performed by a *mohel,* a person skilled in circumcising infants. By tradition, a mohel was assumed to be a man, but more recently, some women have also trained to fill this role.

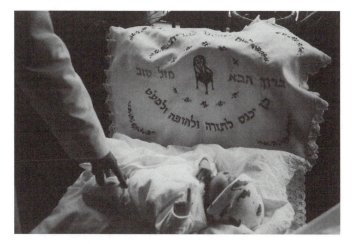

This eight-day-old baby boy is ready for his brit, the ritual circumcision ceremony that welcomes him into the covenant of Abraham. The embroidered letters on the pillow cover say "Welcome" and "Good Luck" (Mazal Tov). Below is the traditional wish: "May you enter into a life of Torah, marriage, and good deeds." Courtesy of the author.

The actual circumcision is only part of the ritual welcoming a baby boy into the covenant of Abraham. The ceremony begins with the baby being carried into the room by the godmother and godfather, two people chosen by the parents to be an important part of the child's life. Sometimes several people are given the honor of carrying the new baby, and he may be passed from grandparents to godparents. Often he is carried on a pillow with a specially embroidered case.

The baby is officially welcomed by the mohel with the Hebrew expression "Barukh haba b'shem Adonai" ("Blessed be he who comes in the name of the Lord"), then handed to the *sandek* or sponsor, whose job is to hold him still while the mohel removes the tiny foreskin. The sandek sits in a chair to the left of an empty chair, often festively decorated. This special seat is set aside for Elijah the Prophet who, according to an old tradition, attends the brit milah of every Jewish child. The mohel, the sandek, and the child's father recite special prayers before the procedure, which usually takes only a few minutes.

When the operation is complete, the baby is given a name. Among Sephardi Jews a child is often named after a living relative, especially a father or grandfather. Ashkenazi Jews consider this a sign of bad luck and will name children only after those who have already died—preferably those who have lived a long life. Both traditions are equally acceptable, as no Jewish law regulates this custom.

Once the new baby has a name, he is usually handed to his mother for comfort and feeding. The parents then recite the traditional blessing heard at many life-cycle events: "Blessed are You, Lord our God, Ruler of the Universe, who has kept us alive and sustained us and brought us to this time." This is usually referred to by the Hebrew word *shehehiaynu* ("who has kept us alive").

The mother and father may also add some words of their own. A common blessing at a brit milah is "Just as he has entered into the covenant, so may he enter into the study of Torah, the marriage canopy, and the performance of good deeds."[2] Until recently, mothers were not expected to attend the brit, but now they are encouraged to participate in this unique commandment.

When the ceremony is complete, the guests call out *"Mazal tov!"* ("Good luck!"). Often, they sing the traditional Hebrew song: *"Siman tov u-mazal tov,"* which means good luck and a good omen. There is general rejoicing and a festive meal usually follows. This may be a small celebration, involving only a minyan of 10 (the minimum number for a brit milah), an elaborate feast with hundreds of guests, or anything in between. It depends on the custom of a particular community, as well as the wealth of the family.

Over the centuries, various reasons have been advanced for not observing the commandment of circumcision. During Hellenistic and early Roman times (from approximately 300 B.C.E. to 200 C.E.), it was frowned upon as a desecration of the perfect male body. In the eighteenth century, the time of the European Enlightenment, circumcision was said to be outdated and unnecessary. At the end of the twentieth century, some doctors were claiming that it had no benefits and was not medically recommended. Still, it persists.

Circumcision has also been outlawed at many different times. In the first and second centuries of the Common Era, the Roman rulers in the land of Israel forbade it, yet Jews risked their lives and continued the practice. Under the rule of the Inquisition in Spain and Portugal, from the fifteenth to the seventeenth centuries, the punishment for circumcising one's son could be death by fire, yet many were circumcised. In Communist Russia during the 1950s, 1960s, and 1970s, Jews were not free to circumcise their children. When they were able to leave the Soviet Union one of their first acts as free Jews was to arrange to have their sons circumcised.

Today, no matter how assimilated Jewish parents may be, or how uninterested they are in Jewish law, few are ready to ignore this ritual. Although a Jew can be Jewish without being circumcised, it is considered the quintessential mark of the Jewish male, the sign of the covenant with God.

In the last decades of the twentieth century and continuing into the twenty-first century, a celebration at the birth has been extended to include girls as well as boys. Although girls are not circumcised, many parents of newborn girls have a party welcoming their daughter into the covenant with special blessings and a ceremony in which the baby girl is assigned godparents, carried in on a pillow, welcomed by the guests, and given a name. This new ritual is called *brit habat*, the covenant of the daughter.

Redemption of the Firstborn

Biblical law says that the firstborn male of every species belongs to God. In ancient times, this meant that the first calf that was born from a cow, the first lamb born from a ewe, or the first kid born from a she-goat was brought to the Temple and sacrificed as a burnt offering to God. This was a token of gratitude to God for granting fertility to the animal who would, presumably, go on to bear other offspring for its owners.

Although the firstborn of humans also technically belonged to God, human infants were never sacrificed. Instead, firstborn sons were redeemed. The Bible (Exodus 13:13–15) explains that the redemption of the firstborn is done to remember the Exodus from Egypt. At that time, God punished the Egyptians by killing their firstborn sons but saved the firstborn of the Israelites. The ritual symbolizing the redemption of the firstborn is called a pidyon haben ("Redemption of the Son") and can be performed any time after the first 30 days of the baby's life. Jews are not supposed to delay in fulfilling a mitzvah (commandment), so the preferred time is therefore the 31st day. It can be postponed for a few days, however, for convenience. The pidyon haben offers another occasion for celebration and festivities.

In ancient times, the redemption of the firstborn simply involved going to the Temple and paying the Kohen (High Priest) five shekels of silver, the amount designated in the Bible (Numbers 18:16). But, the Temple was destroyed more than two thousand years ago, so another ceremony developed to replace that simple act. A Kohen, a descendant of the group who were once designated as priests to serve in the Temple, is now called to the home or to a place chosen by the family. The father hands him the baby and says: "This my firstborn is the firstborn of his mother and God has given command to redeem him." He then repeats the verse from the Torah (Numbers 18:16). For his part, the Kohen asks: "What is your preference? To give me your firstborn son or to redeem him for five shekels?" The father then indicates his preference to redeem his son and gives the five shekels of silver or its equivalent. The parents then recite the Shehehiyanu and the Kohen blesses the child.[3]

Unlike the brit milah, the redemption of the firstborn was required only for specific male children: those who were the first from their mother's womb. If a mother previously had a stillborn child or even a miscarriage, the first living child is not considered a firstborn and need not be redeemed. Children of Kohanim (plural of Kohen) did not have to be redeemed either.

In the United States, the ritual of redeeming the firstborn was practiced mainly among the more observant Jews. In the last decades of the twentieth century, however, with an awakening interest in Jewish ritual by the more liberal branches of Judaism, it has become more popular. It is still limited to firstborns, but it has expanded among some groups of Jews to include firstborn baby girls as well. It is then called a pidyon habat, redemption of the daughter.

Coming of Age: Bar/Bat Mitzvah

Bar mitzvah is another ritual once observed solely for sons but now broadened to include daughters. It is then called bat mitzvah. The term literally means a son (*bar* in Aramaic, the equivalent of the Hebrew *ben*) or daughter (*bat*) of the commandment, implying that the young person has reached religious maturity and is now responsible for following Jewish law as an adult.

The ceremony of bar mitzvah is not found in the Bible. It is first mentioned in the Talmud (Pirkei Avot 5:21) where the age of 13 years and 1 day for boys and 12 years and 1 day for girls is set as the time at which one is obligated to fulfill all the commandments. Until that time, a father is still responsible for the deeds or misdeeds of his children.

There is no evidence that bar or bat mitzvah involved a major celebration during the Talmudic Era (200–600 C.E..) or the early Middle Ages (700–1200). In the thirteenth century, the first mention is seen of boys of 13 being called up to the Torah to say the blessing. At this time, the father would recite "Blessed be God who has freed me from the responsibility for this boy."[4] The young man was now responsible for his own behavior. He was also eligible to be counted in a minyan of 10 men required to recite prayers as a community.

But even after the thirteenth century, for many 13-year-old boys the event was marked simply by putting on tefillin for the first time. Tefillin consist of two small leather boxes containing the complete Sh'ma prayer (see also Chapter 4). The boxes are attached to black leather straps and observant Jews place one on the forehead and wrap the other around the left arm (the arm nearest to the heart) while reciting weekday morning prayers. The reason for this is to literally fulfill the biblical injunction: "You shall bind them as a sign upon your hand and they shall be as frontlets between your eyes" (Exodus 13:9 and Deuteronomy 6:8). Although only observant Jews still follow the ritual of putting on tefillin every morning, most boys (and sometimes girls, as well) learn how to do it before bar mitzvah.

Not until the seventeenth or eighteenth centuries were other specific ceremonies recorded for bar mitzvah boys.[5] In Germany and Eastern Europe, the boy might read a portion of the Torah and the Haftarah (the designated chapters from the Prophets) and lead parts of the service. Male relatives were given the honor of being called to the Torah at this time. At the end of the service, the rabbi blessed the boy and a festive meal was held to celebrate the occasion. These traditions quickly spread throughout the Jewish world.

Traditionally, a boy begins to wear a tallit and tefillin at his bar mitzvah. This young man is practicing for the big day. Courtesy of the author.

In modern times, boys study for several years to attain the skills necessary to chant the portion in the traditional way and recite at least some of the prayers. And no bar mitzvah is complete without a celebration involving family and friends and a festive meal, although elaborate, catered parties marking this occasion are a very recent addition to the ritual.

In the past, there were no rituals to mark the bat mitzvah of a girl. This was, in part, because according to Talmudic law, girls were not obligated to perform most of the commandments. Those commandments that girls (and women) had to follow did not involve synagogue ritual; they were home-centered and were learned not from rabbis or teachers, but from mothers or other female relatives. Once a girl became a bat mitzvah, she was required to say the blessing when lighting the Sabbath or holiday candles. She also had to know and follow all the rules of preparing kosher foods, and observe the laws of *niddah. Niddah* ("one who is excluded") refers to women keeping separate from men during the time of menstruation. Seven days after the end of her menstrual period, a woman must immerse in a ritual bath (*mikveh*). The word niddah is usually translated in more general terms as "family purity." While only a small percentage of modern Jewish women still observe this commandment carefully, it is considered an important part of Jewish law and one of the principal laws required of women.

Actual celebrations marking a girl's coming of age were not recorded before the nineteenth century. They were officially introduced in Germany and France and spread to other countries quite quickly. At first, the ceremony in the synagogue did not involve the girl in any way. Her male relatives were called up to the Torah and she might be given a special gift. With the establishment of Reform Judaism in the early nineteenth century, some girls were given a better education, including lessons in Hebrew, and were confirmed at the age of 16 or 17.[6]

Confirmation was an innovation of the Reform Movement, and during the nineteenth century it was offered as an alternative to bar mitzvah for both boys and girls. However, most Jews, even those who were not religious or traditional, wanted a traditional bar mitzvah for their sons and Confirmation never became popular. Today, Reform synagogues offer Confirmation at 16 or 17, in addition to bar/bat mitzvah at age 13.

Gradually, during the late nineteenth and early twentieth centuries, girls as well as boys were taught to chant the Haftarah and recite specific prayers during the service. But it was still not considered acceptable for girls to be called to the Torah, and girls became bat mitzvah at Friday night services where the Torah was not read.

It was only in the United States that this barrier was finally removed. In 1922, Judith Kaplan, a 12-year-old girl and the oldest of the four daughters of Rabbi Mordecai Kaplan (see also Chapter 6) was called to the Torah to recite the blessing in her father's synagogue.[7] Other congregations were slow to follow that example, but by the mid-1950s, more and more girls were becoming bat mitzvah in Reform and Conservative synagogues. The bat mitzvah itself was set at 13 for girls, too, and they were now offered an education equal to that of boys. Although Friday evening remained a common time to celebrate a bat mitzvah, a growing number were allowed to have a Saturday morning ceremony and were called to the Torah.

By the 1980s, Orthodox Jews were beginning to follow this new tradition of celebration for girls. In Orthodox synagogues, Jewish girls are not called to the Torah and are not able to participate with the men in the traditional service. They are now often educated in Jewish law, however, and their coming-of-age (the bat mitzvah) is celebrated when they reach the age of 12, as stipulated in the Talmud. In some synagogues, the girl is allowed to give a talk, usually an interpretation of the Torah portion, standing in the women's section, either on Friday evening or Saturday morning. Sometimes, the bat mitzvah is conducted at an all-female service, a Women's Tefillah (Prayer) Group, or Women's Minyan. In these all-female settings, Orthodox girls can be called to the Torah to read and say the traditional blessings.

Women's prayer groups were first organized in the 1980s and have spread to many cities in the United States. They offer an opportunity for more traditional women and girls to learn the synagogue skills that men learn and to enjoy the experience of full participation in prayer services. Although many Orthodox denominations do not accept such groups, they are a growing phenomenon in the United States.

Marriage

Marriage is perhaps the most important rite of passage in Judaism because it enables a couple to follow the biblical commandment to "be fruitful and multiply." Because of this, Judaism considers marriage itself to be "the prototypical act of creation."[8]

Traditionally, a Jewish father was expected to find mates for his children, and throughout the ages most Jewish parents were anxious to fulfill that obligation while they were still alive and well. Partly for this reason, Jews tended to marry young. Up until the end of the Middle Ages, it was not unusual for children to be betrothed and even married before puberty, although this was not considered ideal. The proper age for a man to marry was between 16 and 22, before his sexuality led him astray and caused him to have sinful thoughts.[9] For a woman, any time after 12 1/2 was considered acceptable. In the early modern period, however, Jews, along with most other ethnic and religious groups, rejected the practice of such early marriages; and since the 1700s, the acceptable age for marriage has increased steadily.

Jewish marriage laws are complicated. An entire tractate of the Talmud (Tractate Ketubbot) is devoted to marriage. Talmudic laws regulate whom one can legally marry, stipulate the safeguards guaranteed to the wife, and lay out the requirements of the husband. In addition, the rabbis of the Talmud imagined all kinds of different situations in marriage and attempted to solve them by creatively interpreting the law.

The *Ketubbah*

The marriage contract (*ketubbah* in Hebrew) is one of the hallmarks of Jewish marriage and every bride is presented with one at her wedding. Although today these contracts are largely symbolic, throughout most of Jewish history they were important and meaningful. The ketubbah listed the amount of the dowry the bride brought into the marriage and the amount the groom promised to his bride in case the marriage was dissolved by divorce or death. The groom's portion was referred to as the ketubbah money. Usually, the dowry and the ketubbah money (or its equivalent in land or goods) were approximately equal.

This arrangement was a protection for the bride. It ensured that she would be able to support herself if she was widowed or deserted. Her dowry technically remained under her control throughout the marriage. Her husband might use it, invest it, or sell it but not without her approval. When he died, it reverted to her and that debt took priority when the sum of his debts was paid off from his estate.

In addition to stipulations of money or goods paid at the time of the marriage, the ketubbah also listed the rights and duties of both parties. Every marriage contract bound the husband to provide his wife with food, clothing and *onah*, a word that is defined as sexual pleasure. This right is unique to Judaism, and Jewish law took it seriously. From the time of the Talmud and continuing into early modern times, law codes insisted that a husband had to be sexually available to his wife and even stipulated how often they

A ketubbah from Mantua, Italy, dated 1737, is one example of the beautiful marriage contracts that were designed by Jews. The ketubbah was traditionally signed by the husband at the time of marriage and given to the wife for safekeeping. Courtesy of the Library of the Jewish Theological Seminary.

should have intercourse, depending on his occupation and whether he traveled far from home. For example, a sailor was obliged to return home every six months and spend one month with his wife. A laborer was expected to sleep with his wife three times a week (Mishnah Ketubbot 5:6).

The wife had obligations as well. She was expected to manage his household, cook his meals, and bear and care for his children. She also had to be sexually available to him exclusively, although he was free to take a second or even a third wife (see also Chapter 3). Any money the wife earned legally belonged to her husband who supported her.

Other responsibilities or privileges might be added to the ketubbah as well. A couple could agree that if the wife worked, she could keep her earnings and would then be responsible for purchasing her own clothing. The choice of where they lived was often granted to the wife in the marriage contract, and the husband sometimes agreed not to take a second wife without the approval of his first wife. All these stipulations were commonly found in *ketubbot* (plural of ketubbah), especially in the Middle East, well past the twelfth century.

While the text of the ketubbah sometimes seems irrelevant and outdated today, the *ketubbah* itself remains an important symbol of a Jewish marriage. Couples often design their own or commission an artist or calligrapher to design one for them. This work of art may then be proudly displayed in their home.

The Wedding Ceremony

Although marriage laws fill many volumes, the marriage ceremony itself is extremely simple. A Jewish wedding does not even require a rabbi. Technically, all that is necessary is a bride and groom, a ring or other object worth a minimum amount that is given by the groom to the bride, the recitation of the blessings of betrothal and marriage spoken by the groom, and two Jewish men to witness the proceedings. Today, Jewish couples are married with a rabbi to satisfy the requirements of the state or country where they live and the use of a rabbi has become traditional, but Jewish law does not require it.

The best known of the traditions associated with Jewish marriage includes standing under the *huppah*, or marriage canopy, and breaking a glass to complete the ceremony. These and many others practices have been added to the basic Jewish wedding over the centuries. Some are unique to particular lands or particular time periods; others have become almost universal, such as the signing of the ketubbah.

Immediately before the ceremony, the groom meets with the rabbi and two male witnesses and signs the ketubbah with all the agreed on stipulations. According to Jewish law, women were not considered fit witnesses, so this brief event was traditionally attended only by a small group of men, usually including the bride's father but not the bride herself. Today, that custom has changed for many liberal Jewish couples. The bride and groom may both sign the ketubbah—in fact, they may both plan what the *ketubbah* will say—and witnesses may be women as well as men. Since the 1970s, in the United States even the rabbi may be a woman.

It is customary for the bride to be "given away" by both her parents and greeted by the groom who brings her under the huppah, the canopy that represents the Jewish home they will create for themselves. The rabbi or person presiding will give the convocation, then recite the formula for be-trothal, the *erusim*, which includes blessing and drinking a cup of wine. The giving of the ring follows, with the groom reciting: "Behold, you are con-secrated to me with this ring according to the laws of Moses and of Israel." Originally, there was only one ring, the one the groom gave to the bride. Since the 1940s, it has become increasingly accepted for the couple to ex-change rings. The bride may then recite the same formula as the groom, or, in more traditional ceremonies, she may recite a passage from the biblical book, The Song of Songs, instead, so as not to preempt a commandment designated specifically for men.

Immediately after giving the ring (or rings), the rabbi reads the text of the ketubbah and then hands the document to the bride. It is hers to keep. At this point, the rabbi may say a few personal words to the couple before reciting the seven traditional marriage blessings. At the end of the proceed-ings, the groom (or occasionally, the groom and bride together) stamps his foot on the glass and shatters it.

This custom is ancient and can probably be traced back to its symbol-ism as the breaking of the woman's hymen, the sign of her virginity. But written records surrounding the custom began only in Talmudic times. It was first reported as a way to tone down the levity and merrymaking at a wedding (Berakhot 30b–31a). By the fourteenth century, Jews explained the breaking of the glass as a memory of the destruction of the Temple. In later centuries, it was said to recall the sadness that must enter every life, or a recognition that the world is still "broken" and needs to be repaired.[10]

After the ceremony is complete, the bride and groom spend private time together. This is called *yihud* from the Hebrew word *yahad* meaning "to-gether." At this time, they break the traditional fast that is required of the bride and groom the day of the wedding. After about 20 or 30 minutes, they join the festive meal and celebrate with their guests.

Additional customs are often part of more traditional marriages. In Sephardi communities, the future bride gets together with her friends and female relatives for a private, prewedding celebration. At this time she is painted with henna, a special dye that is said to ward off the evil eye.

Just before the ceremony, more observant couples may have individual receptions of their own. After the signing of the ketubbah, the groom re-ceives his male friends and relatives at a special wedding table where they witness the exchange of a small item, usually a handkerchief given by the rabbi to the groom. The groom's acceptance of this object symbolizes his agreement to take on the responsibilities of a husband. The groom is then expected to offer some words of Torah to his guests. Often, he is led to the "groom's table" with music and dancing, and the words of Torah become a comic relief and an entertainment for the guests.

At the same time, the bride receives her female friends and relatives in a separate room. She is seated on a beautifully decorated chair, flanked by her mother and her future mother-in-law. Before the wedding begins, the groom is brought in to see her. This may be the first time the bride and groom have seen each other in several days. The groom now makes sure that the woman is his intended bride. After affirming her identity, he places the veil over her face. This veiling ceremony, called a *bedeken* in Yiddish, is a reminder of the wedding of the biblical Jacob and Rachel. Because Jacob did not see his bride before the wedding, he first married Leah, the wrong sister (see also Chapter 1).

During the wedding ceremony itself, the bride sometimes circles the groom, either on the way to the huppah or under the huppah. This may be repeated either three times or seven times. Although it is not required by Jewish law, circling is a very old custom, probably stemming from the idea that it was a form of protection from evil spirits. Today, this custom is explained by symbolically comparing the bride's circles around the groom with the creation of a new family circle.

Among observant families, the wedding celebration is extended for seven days, one day for each of the seven blessings of marriage. Every evening, the newly married couple is invited to someone's home, usually a relative or close friend, for a meal and the repetition of the blessings.

Divorce

Like the laws of marriage, the laws of divorce are also described and elaborated in a full tractate of the Talmud: Tractate Gittin (divorces). The underlying assumption of Gittin is that marriage is a commandment, not a sacrament. In other words, it is a contract made between humans, not between humans and God. Therefore, although the Talmud says, "when a marriage is dissolved even the altar sheds tears" (Gittin 90b), Jews are nevertheless realistic about the limitations of marriage, and divorce is relatively easy—at least for the man.

A man can divorce his wife at will by giving her a bill of divorcement. This ruling is stipulated in the Bible (Deuteronomy 24:1–4) and does not place any limitations on the grounds for divorce. For a woman, obtaining a legal Jewish divorce (a *get*) is more difficult and complicated because she herself has no right to initiate divorce. She can apply to the Jewish Court (bet din), but they will grant her divorce only for certain very specific reasons, mainly if her husband is sexually impotent or if she finds his profession unbearably distasteful.[11] Even in those cases, however, the husband can refuse the request of the Court. In that event, the woman is considered an *agunah* ("a chained woman"). She is not free to remarry unless her husband agrees to give her a divorce. The man, however, technically can marry another woman without granting his first wife a legal Jewish divorce, although this is not usually accepted within the Jewish community.

The inherent unfairness of Jewish divorce law has plagued Jews through the centuries, and today, with divorce more prevalent than ever, Jews of all denominations have attempted to solve this problem. In general, the Reform Movement recognizes a civil divorce and does not require a get. The Conservative Movement attempts to maintain the traditional law but still protect the woman. They do this by writing a clause into the ketubbah in which the husband agrees that if the marriage is dissolved civilly, he will go to a Jewish Court and give his wife a religious divorce as well. Such a clause can also stipulate that a wife may initiate the divorce. The Orthodox denominations believe that this is not acceptable according to Jewish law and are still struggling with possible solutions.

Intermarriage

Until recently, marriage between Jews was the only marriage recognized by Jewish law and by Jews in general. Rabbis consistently refused to marry a Jew and a non-Jew, claiming that those marriages were illegal. In fact, it was not only Jewish law that deemed them illegal. In Christian lands, marriage to a Jew was illegal for many centuries. The only way a Jew could marry a non-Jew was if he or she converted to Christianity. By the twentieth century, most of those laws were ignored, but in traditional Jewish homes, children who made the choice to "marry out" were seen as rejecting their own people and their own families.

By the mid-twentieth century, however, intermarriage had become so prevalent that accommodations had to be made. Today many Reform rabbis will marry a Jew and a gentile. Sometimes the ceremony is performed jointly by a Reform rabbi and a Christian priest or minister, or by a lay minister. Conservative and Orthodox Jewish clergy still refuse to perform weddings between a Jew and a non-Jew but often do accept the couple once they are married. Sometimes, the non-Jewish spouse converts to Judaism, either before or after the wedding, thus adding to the Jewish people.

Death and Mourning

Nowhere is ritual more important than at times of death and dying, and Judaism supplies a broad panoply of religious rituals and traditions to lead Jews through this crisis. The rituals begin at the time of death itself, when a deathwatch is recommended out of respect for the dying person. As soon as death occurs, the body of the deceased is washed and laid out. This is usually done by a group of Jews called the *Hevra Kadisha,* the "Holy Society," who are knowledgeable about Jewish requirements for the dead. They clean the body and recite prayers asking God to forgive the sins of the person in their care. Then the corpse is dressed and watched over until the time of the funeral.

Even the dressing of the corpse involves specific rules and regulations, reminding Jews that death is a great equalizer. Judaism asserts that both the rich and the poor are equal before God, so all are dressed the same in death. The shroud or garment should be white and made of simple, inexpensive fabric. In addition, male Jews are usually draped in a tallit (prayer shawl) with one fringe cut. This is to signify that he can no longer obey God's commandments.

In most countries, a Jew is buried in a simple coffin of wood, thus fulfilling the principle found in Genesis 3:19: "For dust you are and to dust you shall return." Because of this biblical law, Jews are not allowed to be embalmed or cremated. In the land of Israel, Jews are buried without any coffin at all so that the body may "return to the bosom of the earth."[12]

The actual burial must be accomplished as quickly as possible, and postponing this is considered dishonoring the dead. Delaying a funeral more than 24 hours after death is permitted only if the day of death falls just before a Sabbath or holiday, or if family members need time to travel to the funeral. The time between the actual death and the burial is considered a very sensitive time for the immediate relatives: the parents, siblings, children, or spouse of the deceased. During those hours or days, the mourner is not expected to follow any of the commandments that are ordinarily required for the celebration of holidays.

One of the best-known rituals at a Jewish funeral, one that can be traced back to the Bible, is the tearing of the garment of the mourner. This symbolizes the tearing of the heart at the loss of a dear one and is usually performed just before the burial, either in the funeral home or synagogue where the funeral service is performed, or at the gravesite itself. Often a black ribbon is attached to the mourners' clothing and torn so that the actual garment is not damaged, but some religious Jews consider this unacceptable.

The funeral itself is usually simple, involving the recitation of psalms, a eulogy, and a prayer called *El Maleh Rahamim,* a Hebrew phrase meaning "God, full of compassion." This is a request for God to grant the deceased "perfect rest beneath the sheltering wings of Your presence." Finally, the immediate family (parents, siblings, children, and/or spouse) recite the Kaddish prayer. The mourners then usually follow the corpse to the cemetery and additional prayers are recited before the actual burial.

It is expected that those who attend the funeral will help to cover the coffin with earth. At most Jewish funerals, mourners take turns with the shovel to honor the dead person. The Kaddish is then recited once more and the close relatives of the deceased file out of the cemetery to the comfort of the other participants who repeat the traditional words: "May the Lord comfort you among all the other mourners of Zion and Jerusalem."[13]

At the home where the *shiva,* the seven days of mourning, is to be observed, it is traditional to have a pitcher of water available at the door, so that those returning from the cemetery may wash their hands. A meal of condolence, usually prepared by neighbors or friends, should be laid out after the funeral service. The meal can consist of any type of food but usually includes bread and hard-boiled eggs, a symbol of the cyclical nature of life. The mourners and other guests are encouraged to eat as a life-affirming act. At this time, a candle is lit; the flame and the wick burn for seven days and are said to represent the soul and body of a human being.

For all seven days of mourning, often referred to as shivah ("sitting"), the mirrors in the home should be covered. This is a very old custom with uncertain origins, but it is attributed to the need to concentrate on the loss and not to be diverted by vanity. The mourners should sit either on the floor or on low stools and should not wear leather shoes. They may not go out during the seven days, either, except to attend Sabbath or holiday services at the synagogue. These customs are not only a reminder of the loss that has occurred; they allow the mourner some tangible action to symbolize that loss.

In traditional homes, it is customary for a minyan to gather each morning and evening for the service. This is a form of comfort to the family of the deceased, and it also enables mourners to stay within the confines of their home and still recite the Kaddish. If a home service is not possible, mourners are permitted to go to the synagogue to pray with a minyan.

Throughout the full week of mourning, friends and relatives usually visit to comfort the mourners. It is customary, at this time, to bring food for the family so they will not have to be distracted by providing for their own meals, but no other gifts are appropriate. Flowers are not sent for a Jewish funeral or at any time after. Contributions to charity are acceptable alternatives, and sometimes the family of the deceased designates particular charities they prefer to honor the memory of their loved one.

The first seven days are the most difficult for the mourner and the time when the most comfort and diversion are needed. It is also the time when the mourner has the most restrictions. Men may not shave and men and women should not attend to any but the most basic requirements of hygiene. They are not allowed to attend celebrations or even study the Torah (except for the Book of Job). After the shivah week, restrictions are eased.

The end of 30 days marks the end of the official mourning period for all deceased relatives except parents. A mother or father is mourned for 12 full months. Mourners are expected to recite the Kaddish prayer as part of a minyan if possible, twice a day, every day, at morning and evening services. Not all Jews are able to, or feel obligated to make such a commitment, but many do. Some stand with the mourners to recite Kaddish only on the occasions when they attend synagogue; others choose different ways to remember.

Traditionally, women were not expected to say the Kaddish for parents or other relatives. Although this is a virtual prohibition for Orthodox Jewish women, most Conservative and Reform Jewish women do accept this obligation, and many attend a minyan regularly to say Kaddish for parents.

HOLIDAYS AND FESTIVALS

Jewish holidays fall into several different categories. Those commanded by God in the Bible are the most important holidays in the Jewish calendar. Postbiblical holidays, those adopted later to commemorate specific events, are less important. There are also secular holidays. These have been declared in modern times and although they are often celebrated or memorialized, they fall outside the requirements of Jewish law.

The Sabbath

The first and most important sacred day mentioned in the Bible is the Sabbath. In Hebrew, it is Shabbat and Yiddish-speaking Jews may refer to it as Shobbes. In both these languages—and in most other languages as well—the word is derived directly from the Hebrew *shabat,* meaning "rest." It is a holiday celebrated from sundown on Friday evening until after dark on Saturday night, and even though it occurs every week, observant Jews consider it the most important of all holidays.

The origins of a Sabbath day of rest are ancient, originating even before biblical times, but it was Judaism that first refined it and made it a day of "physical rest and spiritual replenishment."[14] On this day, the Jew is obligated to desist from work so as to remember that God created the world in six days and rested on the seventh. (Genesis 2:1–3). "Remember the Sabbath and keep it holy" (Exodus 20:8) is the fourth of the Ten Commandments.

The sages who compiled the Mishnah outlined 39 types of labor that were forbidden on the Sabbath (Mishnah Shabbat 7:2) These include everything from hard labor such as plowing, hunting, and building, to simple tasks like tying or untying, extinguishing or kindling fire. Later rabbis expanded and explained these prohibitions as involving tasks that create or transform something. Kindling a fire creates light and is thus not allowed. Grinding grain transforms grain into flour and is also forbidden. Any form of transportation is generally forbidden and religious Jews always walk to synagogue on the Sabbath. This practice may be difficult for many modern Jews, who no longer live in small Jewish communities near a synagogue. The Reform, Conservative, and Reconstructionist movements allow Jews to drive to services.

But Sabbath is much more than prohibitions. Beautiful rituals and customs have developed over the centuries to help Jews observe and enjoy this day. It begins with the lighting of the Sabbath candles on Friday evening before dark. This is usually done by the woman of the house, and a special blessing is recited: "Blessed are You, Lord our God, Ruler of the Universe, who blessed us with the commandments and commanded us to light the Sabbath lights." Candle lighting is one of the commandments that women are obliged to perform, but if there is no woman present, the obligation falls on a man.

Those who go to synagogue participate in *Kabbalat Shabbat* ("Receiving Sabbath"). This service takes place at sunset on Friday and officially welcomes Shabbat. One of the special songs sung during the Kabbalat Shabbat service compares the day of rest to a beautiful bride who is ushered in with music and terms of endearment. "Come, bride; come my beloved queen;" they sing, "let us receive the face of the Sabbath."[15]

After this service, there is a festive dinner. According to Jewish law, all meals begin with blessings on the bread and wine and end with the Birkat

On Friday evening, the beginning of the Sabbath, Jews from all branches of Judaism come to pray at the Western Wall, the only remaining remnant of the ancient Temple of Jerusalem. Courtesy of the author.

haMazon, a long blessing thanking God for the food that was just eaten. The Sabbath meal is no exception. Traditionally, this is a joyful meal with a much longer blessing on the wine. This blessing, called Kiddush ("Sanctification") in Hebrew, recalls the six days of Creation and the seventh day when God rested.

There is also a special kind of Sabbath bread, made with white flour and eggs and called *hallah* (sometimes spelled *challah*). Custom demands that on Friday night, two loaves of hallah are set on the table and blessed, one for that evening and the other for the next day. This is an acknowledgment that, when the children of Israel were wandering in the desert, God supplied them with enough mannah on Fridays to last for two days so they would not have to collect it on the Sabbath. During and after the meal, Sabbath songs are often sung.

For observant Jews, the centerpiece of the Sabbath morning is the Shabbat service. It usually begins early, and lasts for several hours, as it includes three parts: the morning service, the Torah service where portions of the Torah and the Prophets (Haftarah) are read, and an additional service (see also Chapter 4). In larger synagogues there may be a choir but usually those in attendance sing the prayers to familiar melodies and are led by a cantor.

The traditional Shabbat service is relaxed and informal. People often arrive late, read the prayers at their own pace, and take time out to talk to friends. Children run in and out and feel at home in the synagogue. Often some small refreshment is served after the service ends. This is called the kiddush because it begins with the Kiddush prayer, the blessing sanctifying the wine.

Sabbath afternoon activities may include lunch, visiting or receiving guests, and studying Torah. True to its original character as a day of rest, for many Jews the Sabbath nap has also become an important part of the observance of this day. Husbands and wives often use this rest time as a time of sexual intimacy. In fact, in the early Middle Ages, Jewish mystics believed that God approved of this Sabbath activity for married couples because it symbolized the perfection of the world.

Sabbath ends with a final meal and the Havdallah service, which can take place in the synagogue as part of the evening service or at home with family and friends. It is a beautiful ritual that marks the division (*havdallah*) between the holy Shabbat and the regular days of the week. It involves a special twisted candle, a box of sweet-smelling spices, and a cup of wine. The wine is blessed and drunk at the beginning of the ceremony. Since Havdallah does not begin until well after sunset, with the appearance of three stars in the sky, the candle signifies the division between light and dark. The spice box is passed around among the participants and represents the sweet smell of the Sabbath, recalling its pleasures for a few more moments. The ceremony usually ends with the singing of "Eliyahu haNavi," a song honoring the prophet Elijah and wishing for his return. According to an old tradition, Elijah is the forerunner of the Messiah and he will appear at the "end of days" (see also Chapter 1). Finally, participants wish each other a good week (Shavua tov) and Sabbath is over.

In the modern Western world, many of these beautiful customs and rituals are ignored, as busy Jews feel obliged to use Saturdays to accomplish tasks for which they have no time during the workweek. A fairly large number of Jews, however, do attempt to keep the Sabbath as a day of physical rest. Even if they do not go to synagogue, they may have a festive Friday evening meal, abstain from work or from everyday chores, and concentrate on recreational activities that refresh the spirit.

The New Year: Rosh haShanah

Rosh haShanah, literally, "the head of the year," falls on the first day of the seventh month (Tishri) of the Hebrew calendar, corresponding approximately to the month of September. Even though it is not in the first month, as one might expect, it is, nevertheless, the Jewish New Year. Both Rosh haShanah and Yom Kippur, the Day of Atonement, are often referred to as "the High Holidays" or "the Days of Awe." They were ordained in the Bible, but little instruction is attached to them, and the actual rules for celebrating these holidays developed long after the Bible was written down.

The biblical book of Leviticus (Leviticus 23:23–25) states only that the first day of the seventh month of Tishri should be a complete day of rest, "commemorated with loud blasts." The book of Numbers (Numbers 29:1–6) repeats the same instructions, calling it "a day when the horn is sounded" and describing the burnt offerings that the Israelites are to make in the Temple on that occasion. Although the Bible stipulated only one day for the observance of this holiday, it came to be celebrated for two days because of the difficulty of ascertaining exactly when the new month (marked by a sighting of the new moon) occurred.

The horn that is sounded on this day is traditionally a shofar, the horn of a ram. It was said to be a remembrance of the biblical story in which Abraham, in obedience to God, went to sacrifice his son Isaac. At the last minute, God sent a ram to replace the boy as a burnt offering.

As time passed, many different customs and meanings were added to Rosh haShanah. According to the Bible it was the Day of Remembering, but exactly what that meant was unclear. More recently, Rosh haShanah is defined as a day to consider the past and to pledge to make the future better. The New Year marks a new beginning and Jews pray for a good and sweet year. At the holiday meal, they dip hallah bread in honey, and eat apples and honey to symbolize sweetness. They are also commanded to bless and eat a new fruit, one never eaten in the past year, to accentuate the newness of the year. To help Jews fulfill that commandment, botanists in Israel create a new fruit each year, often by crossing different species.

It is common among many communities of Sephardi Jews to hold a Rosh haShanah seder, a ritual meal marked by the eating of special fruits and other foods, each having a symbolic value. A blessing is said over each item, all relating to the hope for a good and successful year.

In the synagogue, Jews ask God to "remember us for life" and "inscribe us in the book of life." These lines are part of the prayer service on this holiday and are included in every siddur, along with the *N'taneh Tokef* ("Let us rehearse the grandeur"), a poem written in the tenth century. The title is simply the first two words of the Hebrew poem itself and subsequent lines create the beautiful and haunting image of God as a shepherd who is

A Shofar (ram's horn) is blown on Rosh haShanah and Yom Kippur, as well as each weekday morning for the month preceding those holidays. This shofar is from Persia and dates from approximately 1840. Courtesy of Temple Israel Museum, Great Neck, New York.

counting the flock as they file past and deciding the fate of each one. In addition to praying for forgiveness, Jews look back to the past and remember God's covenant with Abraham, Isaac, and Jacob and all the times when God saved Israel from destruction. The customary greeting on Rosh haShanah is, "May you be inscribed in the book of life."

The most exciting part of the Rosh haShanah service is the blowing of the shofar, done four times throughout the various prayers and readings. In Orthodox synagogues the shofar is also blown at the end of the service. There are specific notes and sequences required for the shofar blasts, each one with a different meaning, and blowing the shofar takes considerable skill and practice. Each synagogue usually chooses a special person for this task. If the holiday falls on the Sabbath, however, the shofar is not blown.

A unique ritual associated with Rosh haShanah, and fitting in with the theme of repentance and a new start, is the ceremony of *tashlikh* probably not practiced before the fifteenth century.[16] Tashlikh ("casting out") involves going to a river or other body of water and throwing crumbs from one's pockets into the moving stream while reciting the appropriate prayer. The crumbs symbolize the sins of the past year that are being cleansed from each individual soul. Tashlikh is performed on the first day of Rosh haShanah unless it falls on the Sabbath. Then it is postponed to the second day.

Days of Penitence

As with almost every holiday in the Jewish calendar, the New Year is marked with festive meals when friends and family gather to celebrate. Candles are lit and blessings recited, but in addition, on Rosh haShanah the process of serious soul-searching and repentance is supposed to begin. The entire month before the holiday, the shofar is blown each weekday, in preparation. Then the Saturday preceding the holiday there is a special midnight service, called Slikhot ("Forgiveness"), which sets the mood for the holiday.

After Rosh haShanah, the 10 days leading to Yom Kippur are called the Days of Penitence and are associated with the image of three books, opened by God on New Year's Day. In the first book are the names of the virtuous, and they will be inscribed for a life of blessing for the next year. In the second book, the names of the wicked are listed. These will surely meet with disaster during the coming year. The third book contains a list of those who have sinned but are redeemable. These people are given a chance to pray for forgiveness and determine their own fate. Most Jews fall into this third category, so the 10 days leading up to Yom Kippur are seen as a last chance for redemption. The devout recite special psalms and prayers each morning during the penitential days, and specific readings are included, reminding God of the times when God's mercy saved Israel from destruction.

The days of penitence end with a strange ritual called Kapparah, meaning "redemption" or "ransom." Traditionally, it occurred before sunrise on the day before Yom Kippur and is a version of a ritual described in the Bible. Leviticus 16 tells how the High Priest, Aaron, must slaughter a goat as a sin-offering for the Israelites before the Day of Atonement. This practice gave rise to the idea of the scapegoat. When the Holy Temple was destroyed and those rituals abandoned, the goat of the sin-offering was replaced by a chicken, a more manageable creature.

Some observant Jews still follow this ritual. A man uses a rooster and a woman a hen. The bird is twirled three times around his/her head while declaring: "This is in exchange for me; this is instead of me; this is as ransom for me."[17] After the ceremony the chickens are killed and sold and the proceeds given to charity. More often these days, the money allocated for charity takes the place of a live animal and the same formula is recited, twirling the package of coins around the head. Although many Jewish authorities have condemned the custom of kapparah, and modern Jews may not even be aware of it, it still persists in some Orthodox circles.

Yom Kippur: The Day of Atonement

Yom Kippur falls exactly 10 days after Rosh haShanah and is, without question, the holiest and most solemn day of the Jewish year. Sometimes called the "Sabbath of Sabbaths" (Leviticus 16:31), it is a fast day, lasting from sunset to sunset during which time Jews are commanded to "do no manner of work" and urged to "cleanse yourselves of all your sins; you shall be clean before the Lord" (Leviticus 16:29–30).

Fasting is one way of purifying the body and soul and also allows the individual to concentrate exclusively on prayer. Traditionally, observant Jews remain in the synagogue the entire evening after sunset, and then again the entire day of Yom Kippur, praying for forgiveness. They pray as individuals, but ask forgiveness as a community. So the prayers ask God: "Pardon us, Forgive us, Grant us Atonement."

One of the most famous prayers, the one that opens the evening service on this holy day, is called *Kol Nidre,* meaning "all vows." The prayer asks God to wipe out all vows made and not fulfilled during the course of the past year and has been widely misunderstood by both Jews and non-Jews. The Kol Nidre prayer certainly does not excuse Jews from keeping promises they have made over the course of the year, or from paying debts owed. It addresses only promises made to God. These promises, and these alone, may be expiated by praying for forgiveness. Any sin committed against human beings can be excused only by correcting the error and asking forgiveness of that person.

The final group of prayers for Yom Kippur is referred to as *Ne'ilah* ("closing"). The image evoked here is the closing of the gates of heaven. This is the last opportunity for penitent Jews to plead their case before God, who decides—in the words of the High Holiday Prayer Book—"who shall live and who shall die; who shall be raised up and who shall be brought low." The holiday ends with a single blast of the shofar; a festive meal is served and a feeling of optimism prevails.

The break-fast, as this meal is called, has become a popular part of Yom Kippur; and sometimes, even Jews who do not attend synagogue services on this holiday, will observe at least a partial fast and end the day with a break-fast, sometimes joining with friends or family. In general, Yom Kippur is widely observed even by those Jews who never attend synagogue at any other time. They may go only for a short time, possibly only to recite the Kaddish, the memorial prayer for the dead, which is included in a special *Yizkor* ("Remembrance") service on this day. Yom

Kippur tends to pull even the most assimilated Jews back to their roots for a short time.

Sukkot: The Feast of Booths

Only five days after the Day of Atonement, Judaism offers another holiday, this one completely different. It is the celebration of the autumn harvest in the land of Israel. *Sukkah* is the Hebrew word for booth or hut and it probably alluded, originally, to the temporary shelters erected in the fields to shelter the harvesters while they gathered the crops. But very early in its history, this holiday took on an additional meaning. The booths (*sukkot*) were said to recall the temporary shelters in which the Israelites lived when God "brought them out of the land of Egypt" (Leviticus 23: 42–43).

The Feast of Booths lasts for one full week, during which Jews were commanded to dwell in the booths. The festival begins and ends with a day of rest when no work is permitted. The intermediate days are considered half-holidays; work is permitted but the commandments concerning the holiday are to continue. These include eating meals in the sukkah and "waving the *lulav*" ("palm frond"). The lulav is the general term for the four species of plants that grow in the land of Israel: the palm frond (lulav), the myrtle, the willow, and the citron (*etrog*), a type of aromatic lemon. These plants are traditionally bundled together and are a symbol of fertility and plenty. Each Jew is obligated to hold the three branches in one hand and the etrog in the other hand, pressed against the base of the branches, and wave them in all directions. This should be done in the sukkah and also in the synagogue (except on Shabbat). At these times, the person recites the traditional blessing, thanking God for the commandments and acknowledging the command of "waving the lulav." There is also a similar blessing when one sits in the sukkah for the first time. While these were originally demanded only for men, nowadays women may wave the lulav and etrog and recite the blessings as well.

The observant Jew begins building his sukkah as soon as Yom Kippur is over. This project often involves the whole family, including small children who decorate the roof with leaves, branches and flowers, fruits, and vegetables. They may draw pictures to hang in their sukkah. Some people sleep in the sukkah, too, although in northern climates this might be difficult.

Jews who live in city apartments may find it impossible to build a sukkah and will try to go to someone who has one so that they can fulfill the commandment at least once during the seven days of the festival. Almost every

On Sukkot, booths are erected and decorated, sometimes even on balconies of apartment houses, to commemorate the festival and the command to dwell in booths. Courtesy of the author.

synagogue finds a way to provide a traditional sukkah for the congregation. A visitor to Israel, or to Jewish neighborhoods in other lands, during Sukkot will notice that booths have been erected everywhere, even on the smallest balconies in urban areas and in the tiniest patches of ground.

Shmini Atzeret: The Day of Assembly

The final day of the Sukkot holiday, Shmini Atzeret, is called in the Bible "a solemn day of assembly" (Numbers 29:35). On Shmini Atzeret Jews gather in the synagogue for a service that includes the Yizkor prayers honoring the dead, and a prayer for rain. The end of the month of Tishri marks the beginning of the rainy season in the land of Israel, so it became the custom to pray for rain at this time, even though, for many centuries, Jews were no longer farmers in the land of Israel. By the mid-twentieth century, the observance of Shmini Atzeret was not common, and was overshadowed by Simhat Torah, a postbiblical holiday (see later), but it remains part of the Jewish calendar of holidays, and observant Jews do not work on that day.

Passover

Yom Kippur may be the most solemn holiday of the Jewish year, but Pesah, the Hebrew word for Passover, is certainly the most popular. Like

Sukkot, Pesah also lasts for a full week but there are no booths. The most important commandment concerning Pesah is that Jews are not allowed to eat any leavened bread during this period. Unleavened bread, or matzah, is bread that has not been allowed to rise with yeast or other leaven before being baked. The Bible explains this prohibition as a reminder of the Exodus from Egypt, because the Jews had to leave quickly and had no time to let their dough rise.

The story explaining Passover can be found in the book of Exodus. It is the story of Moses and how he led the Israelites out of Egypt (see also Chapter 1). The story of the Exodus from Egypt is such an intrinsic part of Judaism that Jews regularly retell it at a unique home ceremony called a seder. *Seder* is a Hebrew word that comes from the same root as the word *siddur* (prayer book) and means "order." But the Passover seder is much more than a service or a series of prayers. It is an attempt to fulfill the biblical injunction that parents must teach their children about the Exodus from Egypt (Exodus 13:8).

The seder begins with four questions that the children ask their parents and then proceeds with the answer. It explains how God took the Israelites "out of the house of bondage," allowed them to cross the sea, protected them while they wandered in the desert for 40 years, and brought them to the land of their forefathers Abraham, Isaac, and Jacob. Added to the story are songs, blessings, and reminders of other times and places where God may have intervened in human affairs. The seder is a ceremony that offers something for everyone, from the youngest children to the most revered elders in the family. And finally, it is a meal full of symbolic foods and rituals with lots of room for innovation. It is held the evening of the first day of Passover and traditionally repeated on the second evening.

As the seder is long and complicated, a book, called the *Hagaddah* ("The Retelling") allows participants to follow along, reading the questions and the story that follows, singing the songs, and reciting the blessings in turn. *Hagaddot* (plural of Hagaddah) have been translated into numerous languages and have evolved in many ways since they began to be used in the first centuries of the Common Era. Today, every branch of Judaism and every geographical and linguistic group of Jews has its own Hagaddah, adding its own unique traditions to the basic story.

The rituals for Passover outlined in the Bible (Exodus 34:25; Leviticus 23:6–8; Deuteronomy 16:16) are relatively simple. It must be celebrated on the fifteenth day of the month of Nissan, roughly in late March or April of our calendar, and includes a pilgrimage to the Temple in Jerusalem, the sacrifice of a lamb, and a family feast, not to be eaten with leavened bread. Since the destruction of the Temple, however, numerous customs have developed to replace the original ones. They were first outlined in the Mishnah, the earliest compilation and explanation of biblical law (Mishnah Pesah 10:4), where the basic questions that form the core of the Hagaddah can already be found. Each generation added rituals and symbols based on its own experiences and ideas. In recent times, prayers and readings have been introduced memorializing those who perished in the Holocaust, honoring the modern state of Israel, and comparing the slavery and freedom of the ancient Israelites with the struggles of African Americans and the Civil Rights Movement.

In spite of all these changes, twenty-first century customs surrounding the Passover holiday are not that different from the customs that were observed for hundreds of years. They begin with the cleaning of all leaven from the house. This is done in the days preceding the holiday and climaxes with a ceremony called *bedikat hametz* ("searching for leaven"). This probably originated with the idea of involving the children in the preparation for the holiday and is essentially a treasure hunt. The adults hide pieces of bread throughout the house and the children, armed with a wooden spoon and feather to sweep away the crumbs, a box to hold the unwanted leaven, and a candle to light up dark corners, set out to find what was hidden. The next morning, the accumulated crumbs and pieces are burned and the fa-

At the Passover seder, a grandfather divides the matzah, the traditional unleavened bread that is eaten on Passover. Courtesy of the author.

ther or other adult declares that "all manner of leaven that may be in my possession should be declared as null and void." Instructions for this ritual with the appropriate blessings can be found in every Hagaddah.

Another ritual that helps to prepare for Passover is the fast of the firstborn. Because God saved the firstborn of the Hebrews while killing the firstborn of the Egyptians, firstborn male Jews are obligated to fast on that day. To avoid fasting, a person can complete the study of a tractate of the Talmud, which demands a celebratory meal. To accommodate those who would like to fulfill this commandment, some synagogues hold early morning study sessions on the day of the first seder, followed by a breakfast.

The preparation of the table for the seder ceremony and meal is in itself a complicated ritual because room has to be made for all the symbolic foods that are eaten. The centerpiece of the ceremonial meal is a seder plate, a round or square platter with six sections in it. There is a place for a roasted egg (a traditional sign of spring), a roasted shank bone (in memory of the lamb that used to be sacrificed in the Temple), a green vegetable (another sign of spring), two forms of bitter herbs symbolizing the bitterness of slavery, and a special mixture of chopped nuts and fruits, mixed with wine. This is called *haroset* and is supposed to look like the mortar that the Hebrew slaves used to make bricks. In addition, there must be three pieces of matzah, and a dish of salt water to represent the tears of the slaves. Each of these is used in the seder itself.

The traditional Hagaddah includes readings and songs to be recited both before and after the meal, as well as the regular blessings and grace after the meal (Birkat haMazon). One popular custom, especially among the children, is the hiding and finding of the *afikomen*. Afikomen is a Greek word that means "dessert." Traditionally, it was a piece of matzah taken from the stack of three matzot on the seder table and required for the official ending of the meal. The person who leads the seder usually hides it for the children to find. When the time comes to distribute the afikomen, the children have a chance to bargain for a prize in return for the matzah so that the meal can end and the seder can be completed. This is a good way of keeping young children awake and alert until the long meal is completed.

In Israel, only one seder is held, but in other lands, because of the original uncertainty of calculating the proper day, two seders (the plural is *sederim*, in Hebrew) are the norm, although Reform Jews celebrate only one. The prohibition against eating "all manner of leaven" continues for the full seven days in Israel and eight days in the Diaspora.

As was the case with Sabbath restrictions, the commandments against "all manner of leaven" were analyzed and expanded in the Talmud to make sure that even the smallest infraction was not inadvertently overlooked. Rabbinic law, therefore, elaborated on the laws of Passover in one full tractate (Pesahin). Gradually, the laws against eating leaven grew to include anything that is fermented, that is, all baked goods made with yeast or baking powder, and anything that might ferment such as vinegar, wine, and cider. Until the twentieth century, these dietary restrictions made Passover a holiday in which feasting was limited. Recently, however, Jews have created an entire industry of "kosher for Passover" foods, including cakes, crackers, and other treats made with flour that has been carefully watched under rabbinical supervision so that it does not ferment. Specially supervised wines and vinegars are also prepared for this holiday and in the United States, major manufacturers of dairy products and soft drinks stamp their products "kosher for Passover" to assure Jews that they contain no flour or leavening.

While many Jews are not strict about abstaining from bread or other products made with leaven, most keep some aspect of the holiday. Even those who do not have a seder will often have a festive holiday meal and will include matzah on the table. Passover is the most celebrated holiday in the Hebrew calendar. The intermediate days are not actual holidays, but on the first and last days of Pesah Jews are commanded not to work and there is a special synagogue service.

Shavuot: The Feast of Weeks

Along with Sukkot and Passover, Shavuot, too, is a harvest holiday and is considered one of the three pilgrimage festivals, times when Jews were supposed to come up to the Holy Temple in Jerusalem and offer a sacrifice to God. These three holidays are also agricultural, marking the seasons in the land of Israel. Sukkot is the fall harvest, Pesah notes the first signs of spring and marks the season of spring planting and barley harvesting, and Shavuot is the festival of the first fruits, in Hebrew: Hag haBikkurim.

The exact meaning of the word Shavuot is "weeks" because 49 days, or 7 weeks are counted from Passover to the spring harvest. Because Shavuot falls on the 50th day, it is also referred to as Pentacost. And observant Jews do literally count the days. Beginning at the end of the second seder, on the second evening of Passover, participants recite: "This is the first day of the omer (sheaf of barley)." After this announcement, the omer is officially counted each evening at sunset, until 49 days have passed.

During these days, observant Jews do not cut their hair, get married, wear new clothes, listen to music, or attend public celebrations. Although many reasons have been offered for this custom, it seems clear that it stems from a very old tradition—the same tradition from which the Christian practice of Lent emanated.[18] The only exception to this state of semi-mourning is the 33rd day of the omer (*Lag b'omer*), when the ban is lifted.[19] For this single day, people may marry, cut their hair, and celebrate.

It is also the custom for children to go into the woods on Lag b'omer, to have picnics and to play with bows and arrows. A Talmudic interpretation attributes this practice to the fact that during the first century of the Common Era, the Romans forbade the Jews from studying Torah. The young scholars defied the authorities by slipping into the woods with bows and arrows to camouflage the fact that they were secretly learning Jewish law. It is clear, however, that the celebration of Lag b'omer is much older than the first century and has its parallels in almost every culture throughout the Middle East and Europe.

According to Deuteronomy (15:9–10), the 49 days of the omer begin "when the sickle is first put to the standing grain" (that is, on the second day of Passover). "Then you shall observe the Feast of Weeks for the Lord your God." Leviticus 23:17 also mentions Shavuot, describing the method of counting. "You must count until the day after the seventh week—fifty days." On the 50th day, the Israelites were commanded to offer a sacrifice to God. Instructions were very specific: "You shall bring an offering of new grain to the Lord." This was followed by precise instructions: two loaves, made with "two tenths of a measure of choice flour" along with burnt offerings.

Once the Temple was destroyed and these offerings to the Lord were no longer possible, Shavuot quickly took on new meaning. It was said to commemorate the time when God gave Israel the Ten Commandments and the Torah on Mount Sinai. Although this new interpretation became part of Judaism only in rabbinic times—the first written mention of Shavuot as the holiday of the Giving of the Law was the third century of the Common Era—it was quickly adopted and became widespread.[20] Thus, all three harvest holidays were eventually tied in to the Exodus from Egypt.

Since the late 1800s and the redevelopment of agriculture by Jews in the land of Israel, Shavuot is celebrated with a simulated pilgrimage to Jerusalem, with children carrying baskets of fruit and barley. For the religious, it is a day of rest and prayers of thanksgiving. For the more secular Israelis, it is a day for pleasure and relaxation.

Outside of Israel, the contemporary celebration of Shavuot lasts for two days instead of one and occurs mainly in the synagogue. There is a special holiday service with designated readings from the Torah and Haftarah and the traditional reading of the biblical Book of Ruth.

Explanations for choosing the Book of Ruth vary. Some rabbis say that because Ruth was a convert, it is appropriate to read about her at the time of the giving of the Law. Another reason is tied to the verses in Leviticus. These verses immediately follow the description of the Shavuot offerings and explain: "And when you reap the harvest of your land, you shall not reap all the way to the edges of the field, or gather the gleanings of your harvest; you shall leave them for the poor and the stranger" (Leviticus 23:22). Ruth, according to the story, came to the land of Israel as a poor stranger. She survived by following the harvesters and picking up the gleanings for herself and her mother-in-law, Naomi.

In the United States, it has become popular to hold an all-night study session on the eve of Shavuot, as a reminder that it is the holiday of the Giving of the Law. A medieval practice common in European countries was to initiate young children into their studies on this day by bringing them to the schoolhouse when they were approximately five years old. The ceremony included giving the children sweets so that they would always associate learning with sweetness. This tradition has been revived in the twentieth century and young children attending the first year of Hebrew School are often presented with their own siddur on Shavuot, followed, of course, by a refreshment of sweets. Shavuot is also a popular time for Reform Jews to hold the Confirmation ceremonies of their post-bar/bat mitzvah students, as it usually falls in late May or June.

It has become customary to eat dairy foods on Shavuot, especially blintzes, a thin pancake stuffed with cheese or fruit. As on almost every other holiday, candles are lit, blessings are recited, and observant Jews do not work.

Purim

The last of the holidays mentioned in the Bible is Purim, an ancient word that means "lots." It is said to come from the fact that lots were cast to decide on which day the Jews of Persia would be destroyed. Although Purim can be traced to the ancient practice of celebrating Carnival halfway between winter and spring, it came to signify something much more meaningful for Jews: the rescue of their people from destruction.

The story of Purim is found in the biblical Book of Esther and takes place in ancient Persia. Esther, a Jewish woman, is chosen by means of a beauty contest, to be a wife to King Ahasuerus. Esther's cousin Mordecai (some say he is her uncle or her guardian) and the King's powerful Vizier, Haman, become rivals. To take revenge on Mordecai, Haman plots to kill all the Jews in the kingdom. Mordecai warns Esther and tells her she must intervene.

Esther fasts to prepare herself, then, at the risk of her life, asks for an audience with the King. It is granted and when she tells him of the plan to kill her people, King Ahasuerus orders Haman and his sons to be killed instead. Although the King cannot legally rescind Haman's decree, he allows the Jews to fight against those who come to kill them and thus save themselves. The Book of Esther ends with the statement: "Consequently, these days are recalled and observed in every generation… . And these days of Purim shall never cease among the Jews, and the memory of them shall never perish among their descendants" (Esther 9:28).

Although there is absolutely no historical verification for this story, Purim has been celebrated on the 15th day of the Hebrew month of Adar (approximately March in the Western calendar) from earliest times and continues to be observed today. It is a time of merrymaking and games. Children, and sometimes adults, dress up as the characters in the Purim story, or in costumes from many different cultures. Gambling and playing cards are popular activities for adults, and Purim balls, humorous plays, and carnivals are widespread both in Israel and in the Diaspora. Even drinking excessively is condoned on Purim, when Jews are supposed to drink "until they do not know the difference between Haman and Mordecai" (Megillah 7b).

The day before Purim is a minor fast day called the Fast of Esther. This recalls the day when Esther fasted in preparation for approaching the King to make her request to save the Jews, but it is not widely practiced today, except by observant Jews.

On the eve of Purim, immediately after the Fast of Esther, Jews gather in the synagogue to hear the story of brave Esther and Mordecai, the foolish King Ahasuerus, and the wicked Haman. Every time Haman's name is mentioned in the reading, the listeners stamp their feet or spin special noisemakers, called *groggers* in Yiddish or *ra'ashanim* in Hebrew, to block out his name. Children wave paper flags with the Hebrew words: "And for the Jews there was light and joy" and general merriment prevails.

A special pastry eaten on Purim is called *hamentaschen* ("Haman's pockets") in Yiddish and *Oznei Haman* ("Haman's ears") in Hebrew. These are three-cornered pieces of cookie or pastry dough stuffed with a filling of prunes, apricots, or poppy seeds. The shape is supposed to represent Haman's hat, but the various names given to this treat belie that theory. Jewish families often bake or buy these small cakes and, together with other treats, send them to friends and family as special Purim gifts. This custom is called *Mishloah Manot* ("the sending of gifts").

Purim is considered a minor holiday. It is celebrated for only one day, and it is not necessary to light candles on this day or abstain from work. But the rescue of Jews from their enemies is especially meaningful for many who, over the centuries, have themselves been rescued from imminent danger. Many communities throughout the world celebrate their own versions of Purim.[21]

POSTBIBLICAL HOLIDAYS

Several holidays included in the Jewish calendar had their origins after the biblical period. Although these are considered less important than those commanded in the Bible, they have taken on greater significance over the centuries and are often extremely popular. Chief among these is the holiday of Hanukkah.

Hanukkah

Although not biblically ordained, the origins of Hanukkah can be traced directly back to the time that the Maccabees revolted against the Syrian-Greeks in 165 B.C.E. Thus, it is the only post-biblical Jewish holiday with a sound historical base. The Maccabean wars are recorded in the Apocrypha, in Maccabees I and II.[22] This war was led by Mattathias and his five sons, a family of kohanim (Jewish priests). The middle son, Judah, was chosen as the military leader. Along with his brothers and an army of followers, Judah managed to defeat the Syrian-Greek forces in what was essentially a civil war between Jews who wanted to adopt Greek/Hellenistic culture and Jews who wanted to maintain a traditional way of life. Against considerable odds, the Jewish army, calling themselves Hasidim ("Pious Ones"), beat back the Syrian army that was supporting the pro-Greek assimilationist Jews. In a series of successful guerilla operations, the Hasidim, led by the Maccabees, defeated King Antiochus IV, ruler of the land of Israel at that time.

After gaining the victory, the Maccabee brothers and their army re-claimed the Holy Temple in Jerusalem, defiled by Syrian soldiers during the course of the war. After cleaning and restoring it, Judah Maccabee declared a weeklong holiday on the 25th of the month of *Kislev* (approximately December). It was called Hanukkah, or Rededication.

The new holiday was originally intended as a substitute for Sukkot, the fall harvest holiday that had not been celebrated that year because of the ongoing war. It took on a life of its own, though, and legends of miracles quickly grew up around those days and captured the popular imagination.

The legend of Hanukkah, as it has come down from the Talmud, relates that when the Jewish soldiers came into the desecrated Temple they sought immediately to rekindle the eternal light, lit with consecrated oil, that always burned above the alter. There was only enough oil remaining to last for a single day, so a soldier was sent to find more. But the single cruse of oil did not go out as expected; it continued burning for eight full days, until new oil was obtained and brought to the Temple.

The lighting of candles for eight days recalls this miracle. The candles are lit in a special candelabrum called a menorah or a *hanukkiah*. It has a place for eight candles, each representing one day of the miracle, plus a ninth candle called the *shammash*, used to light the other candles. Only one candle (plus the shammash) is lit on the first night of Hanukkah, two on the second and so on, until the eighth day when all are lit. The lighting ceremony takes place at sundown, the traditional start of each day, and blessings are chanted while the candles are lit. The first blessing is the same as the blessing for Sabbath or holiday candles; the second one blesses God "who made miracles for our ancestors in those days and in this time." Hanukkah songs customarily follow the blessings.

It has also become the custom on Hanukkah to play with spinning tops called *dreidls* or *s'vivonim*. This is a game played with a four-sided top in which players take out or put in pennies, nuts, or other symbolic currency, according to how the top falls. On each side is a Hebrew letter, said to be the initials of the four Hebrew words: *Nes gadol haya sham* ("a great miracle happened there"). Since the establishment of the state of Israel, that sentence has been changed to "a great miracle happened *here*," and initials on Israeli-made tops reflect that change.

In Israel, Hanukkah is marked by a torch relay race, beginning in the town of Mod'in, the birthplace of the Maccabees. Candles are lit each night and foods cooked in oil are eaten. In Israel and other Middle-Eastern lands,

A family participates in lighting the Hanukkah candles. Courtesy of the author.

the traditional food for this holiday is jelly donuts; in Europe it is potato pancakes. American Jews, whose origins are varied, may chose one or the other. Hanukkah is not a holiday during which Jews are required to rest. Work continues as usual in between the parties and the candle lighting.

Giving gifts to children on Hanukkah is relatively recent and occurs mainly in the United States. In other countries of the Diaspora, it was sometimes the custom for adults to give children small coins during the holiday. In Eastern Europe, where Yiddish is spoken, this was called Hanukkah *gelt* (the Yiddish word for "money"). In parts of the West, especially the United States and Canada where elaborate Christmas gifts are an important tradition, toys and other gifts began to be offered to Jewish children as well, partly to offset the appeal of Christmas, which falls at approximately the same time. Because of this practice, Hanukkah is often considered by non-Jews to be the Jewish Christmas. This is certainly not the case. Although both holidays can trace their ancient roots back to prebiblical times, when fires and lights were lit at the time of the winter solstice, they have taken on very different meanings today. Hanukkah celebrates the victory of the few over the many, confirms the Jewish idea that God intervenes in the affairs of human beings, and commemorates one of the earliest struggles to maintain cultural and religious diversity at a time when that was certainly not the norm.[23]

The Holiday of Rejoicing in the Law: Simhat Torah

Observance of a holiday called Simhat Torah was not recorded until after the Talmudic period, which ended in the early part of the sixth century C.E., but it is actually an extension of Sukkot. It is celebrated in the Diaspora on the second day of Shmini Atzeret and in Israel on the same day as Shmini Atzeret, usually in late September or early October. This holiday probably began in the period of the gaonim, the heads of the great academies of the Middle East, although some say it began in Western Europe.[24]

The reason for the holiday was a change in the original custom of completing the reading of the Torah over the course of three years. When this was changed to one year, the new, annual cycle meant that the reading of any particular passage would fall on the same week every year. It also meant that the Torah reading would always be completed at the end of Sukkot. With this new, shorter cycle, it became customary not only to complete the reading on this day, but to immediately start reading it again. In an attempt to include every single Jew in the celebration and to acknowledge the importance of Torah in the life of the Jews, some very special traditions developed, making this one of the most beloved of all synagogue festivities, perhaps second only to Purim.

The holiday is celebrated in the synagogue, with all the scrolls of the Torah taken out of the Holy Ark and carried around the room in a procession. Smaller synagogues may have only a few Torah scrolls, but larger synagogues often have a dozen or more. The scrolls are covered with beautiful coverings of velvet, decorated with embroidery. They are often ornamented with silver filigree and silver medallions. In communities of the Middle East, many Torahs have solid cases made of fine filigreed silver.

The Torahs are carried around the synagogue seven times, each time by different people, while the congregation sings and dances along, often becoming very exuberant. In many synagogues, the procession spills out into the streets. In Israel, Simhat Torah celebrations are held in public parks so that all the citizens, including those who do not go to synagogue, can participate. Everywhere that Jews observe this holiday there is joy and singing. Children wave special paper flags, sometimes with apples stuck on top and lighted candles inside the apples. The light is said to represent the light of the Torah, the light of learning.

After seven *hakafot* (circuits) are completed and the dancing, singing and rejoicing have quieted down, the Torah is read. The honor of either reading the Torah portions on this day or saying the blessings before and after those portions are read, usually goes to important people in the congregation. The person who is called up for the very last lines of Deuteronomy, the last of the five books of the Torah, is called the *hatan* Torah or "bridegroom of the Torah." The person who follows, reads the first lines of Genesis and is called hatan Bereshit. Bereshit is the Hebrew name for "Genesis," the first book of the Torah. Some synagogues add a third person to be honored by reading the Haftarah, the passage from the Prophets. Each of these honorees is escorted by other synagogue or family members of his or her choice. They bring the honoree up to the *bimah*, the platform where the Torah is read, while the cantor chants special songs.

Traditionally, only men were called to the Torah. Women were not even permitted to carry the Torah in the traditional circuits around the synagogue. This is still the case in most—but not all—Orthodox synagogues, where women sit in a separate section and can only watch the festivities.[25] In Reform and Reconstructionist synagogues, and in most Conservative synagogues, women are now allowed full equality. They may carry the Torah and are also sometimes called up for the last or first lines of the readings. If a woman is given that honor, she is called a *kallat* Torah ("a bride of the Torah") or kallat Bereshit ("bride of Genesis").

Simhat Torah is the only time when children can participate in the Torah service. The custom of giving children younger than 13 a special aliyah (the honor of being called up to the Torah) is practiced in most synagogues. They are called up as a group, while the adults hold the four corners of a tallit (a fringed prayer shawl) over their heads. A respected congregant is chosen to chant the blessing for them and a short portion of the Torah is read. After the concluding blessing is recited, the rabbi blesses the children.

After the Torah reading, the traditional musaf (additional) service is sung, with special hymns added for this holiday. As on most other holidays, no work is permitted on Simhat Torah.

Tishah b'Av and Other Minor Fasts

Tishah is the Hebrew word for "nine" and Av is one of the months in the Hebrew calendar, usually corresponding to August. So Tishah b'Av simply denotes the ninth of Av. Most Jews who are even slightly observant, however, understand more than that simple meaning when they hear Tishah b'Av mentioned. It is a day of mourning, a day that commemorates the destruction of the First Temple by the Babylonian King Nebuchadnezzar in 586 B.C.E. and the end of an independent Jewish state.

Tishah b'Av has come to symbolize all the tragedies that have befallen the Jewish people over the centuries. It is believed to be the day that both the First and Second Temples were destroyed. The Bar Kokhba rebellion, the last attempt by Jews to regain their independence from the Romans, was supposedly put down on that day.[26] Later in Jewish history, the expulsion of the Jews from Spain was said to have occurred on the ninth of Av, but this date was a fast day even in biblical times and this was confirmed in the Mishnah and the Talmud.

Observant Jews abstain from food from sunset to sunset on Tisha b'Av and may decide not to eat meat from the beginning of the month of Av. They also follow other customs that are associated with mourning: mourners sit either on the floor or on low stools; are not allowed to bathe, shave, or wear new clothes; and do not wear leather shoes. Even studying Torah is forbidden on that day, as study is considered a joyful activity.

On the evening that Tishah b'Av begins, there is a special service, often with lit candles rather than electric lights. In some synagogues the congregants sit on the floor. The feature of the Tishah b'Av service is the reading of the biblical Book of Lamentations, a total of five chapters that mourn the destruction of Jerusalem. The opening verses are:

"Alas!
Lonely sits the city
Once great with people!
She that was great among nations
Is become like a widow." (Lamentations 1:1)

The end of the fifth chapter was especially meaningful to Jews who had just lost their land and their independence: "Our heritage has passed to aliens/Our homes to strangers" (Lamentations 5:2). Finally, the very last lines were an appeal to God: "Renew our days as of old! For truly, you have rejected us" (Lamentations 5:21–22).

The entire book is read in a mournful chant, used only on this day. The following morning, special dirges are included in the regular weekday service and men do not wear the traditional tallit or put on tefillin because these are considered adornments.

In modern Israel, many shops and places of entertainment are closed on Tishah b'Av, but outside of the observant community, most Israeli Jews do not fast. After the 1967 War, when Jerusalem was reunited, there was even some question about whether this day of mourning should continue to be observed. The decision was made to continue, although some suggest an alteration in the ritual.[27]

Outside of Israel, Tisha b'Av is ignored by many Jews, but a large portion note it, either by attending synagogue services, fasting, or just abstaining from meat. Reform Judaism once rejected this holiday as no longer appropriate for Jews, but more recently, they have returned to it, reinterpreting it so that it is relevant for modern times.

Besides Tisha b'Av there are three other fast days that are noted in the Hebrew calendar, also without any specific name other than the day and the month: the 10th of Tevet, the 17th of Tammuz, and the 3rd of Tishri. These fasts probably date back to ancient fast days relating to harvest times, but each was later associated with a specific event tied to the fall of the Temple. They are rarely commemorated today except by the most observant, and most Jews are unaware of them.

Tu B'Shevat: The New Year of the Trees

Tu b'Shevat, or the 15th of the month of Shevat, was first mentioned in the Mishnah, although it probably started before that as a popular folk holiday. It is another holiday that recalls the agricultural cycle in the land of Israel, a day "when the sap begins to rise in the fruit trees" and the first signs of spring appear.[28] Although the month of Shevat corresponds approximately to January or February in our calendar, that is the season when new trees are planted in Israel and so it is called the New Year of the Trees.

For centuries, even after Jews were exiled and lived in other climates, they remembered this day and observed it by eating the fruits of trees native to their ancient homeland. Often, the fruits were eaten dried, because they were not available any other way. Dried figs, dates, apricots, and almonds were commonly eaten on Tu b'Shevat, as well as a dried, podlike fruit called carob or St. John's bread.

Once Jews began to return to the land of Israel in the late 1800s, and to work the land, they could once again plant trees in the proper season. And because in those years the land was still largely barren, it became the custom for Jews living in the Diaspora to contribute money for trees that were planted in their names. In this way, whole forests grew up in modern Israel. In the twenty-first century, Jews still send money to plant trees in honor or in memory of a loved one.

On Tu b'Shevat, the New Year of the Trees, children plant trees on the hills outside Jerusalem. Courtesy of the author.

Dried and fresh fruits continue to be eaten on Tu b'Shevat, both in Israel and in the Diaspora, and a Tu b'Shevat seder has become a popular tradition. This ceremony was common among Sephardi Jews but has been adopted by Ashkenazi Jews as well. It involves special blessings and prayers to be recited over each fruit in turn: the pomegranate, the apple, the almond, the carob, and the mulberry. Each of the fruits has a symbolic meaning. In recent times, other fruits are sometimes added as well. The Tu b'Shevat seder is a joyous reminder that the land of Israel is once again a fertile place where Jews are free to practice their own traditions and live under their own laws.

There is no requirement to abstain from work on Tu b'Shevat, and Jews tend to forget it; however, it is celebrated widely in the United States by children who attend Hebrew school. In Israel, it has become similar to Arbor Day. Teachers and youth leaders bring children out to the fields to plant new trees and feel close to nature just as the new growth of spring is about to appear.

New Moons

Judaism follows a lunar calendar, so each month begins when the first sign of the new moon appears in the sky. That day is called Rosh Hodesh, literally, "the head of the month." The full moon always comes in the middle of the month and the month ends as the moon wanes and disappears. In the synagogue, each month is heralded with special prayers on the Sabbath preceding the appearance of the moon. Just as the moon renews itself every four weeks, Jews pray for their own renewal and for pardon of their sins. This prayer is a substitute for the burnt offerings that the ancient Israelites brought to the Temple every month.

Rosh Hodesh is not a day of rest, but in centuries past it was the custom for women to do less work than usual on this day. Such a half-holiday was considered a special reward because in the past, women had contributed their gold jewelry to decorate the Tabernacle, built to hold the Ten Commandments.

The custom of giving women a half-holiday once a month fell into disuse at least a century ago, but Jewish feminists have brought it back as a day particularly meaningful to women. They have organized Rosh Hodesh study groups where women can come together, study Jewish law, and feel empowered to expand their place in Judaism.

SECULAR HOLIDAYS

Since Israel became a Jewish state in 1948, the country has established several holidays or holy days in addition to those described in the Bible or in later books of Jewish law. These are not considered religious holidays because they recall political events. Nevertheless, many Jews, both inside and outside of Israel, do celebrate or commemorate them.

Yom HaShoah and Yom HaZikaron

Yom haShoah and Yom haZikaron both fall in the month of Nissan, usually late April or early May, and are among the saddest days in the Jewish calendar. Yom haShoah is Holocaust Memorial Day, the day to commemorate the six million Jews who were killed by the Nazis during World War II. While this holiday is not part of the religious calendar, special services, prayers, and readings in synagogues all over the world mark Yom haShoah. Events are set up not only to memorialize those who died but also to honor those who survived. Jews remember the Holocaust and the murder of their people not because they want to glorify their suffering. They believe it is important for all people to learn from this terrible event and make sure it never happens again, either to them or to any group of people in the world.

The day after Holocaust Memorial Day is Yom haZikaron, or Remembrance Day. Yom haZikaron is commemorated mainly in Israel and is very much like Memorial Day in the United States. On that day, sirens wail at a set time, and all stop what they are doing to observe a minute of silence in honor of the soldiers who died in the wars defending Israel. Because Israel is such a small country and most young people, boys and girls, are required to serve in the army, almost everyone knows someone who was killed fighting to protect their homeland. Israelis take Yom haZikaron very seriously and no matter what they are doing or where they are going, the entire population of the country is at a standstill for that one moment.

Yom HaAtzma-ut: Independence Day

Coming exactly one week after Holocaust Memorial Day, Yom haAtzma-ut (Independence Day) is the happiest of the secular holidays. It marks the day when the United Nations voted to approve the establishment of a Jewish state and the new state of Israel declared its independence. This happened on the fifth day of the month Iyyar and usually falls in late April or early May.

In the early years of the new state, it was customary to have a big parade, proudly displaying Israel's brand new army, air force, and navy. Israeli planes would fly in formation over the parade ground, dipping and trailing smoke. Bands played and young soldiers in uniform showed off their marching formations before a crowd of thousands of citizens and tourists. After the 1967 War, and Israel's major victory over the neighboring Arab armies, this parade was discontinued, but there is still a great deal of gaiety in the streets on Yom haAtzma-ut. Music plays and children run around wielding small plastic hammers that squeak when someone is tapped with them and swing wind toys that spin around and make a high-pitched sound. It is an occasion for parties and dancing in the streets.

A very short time after Israel's independence, Jews around the world began to celebrate this day as well. They recite psalms and other prayers of thanks in the synagogue. Communal Jewish organizations often make parties for their members or celebrate with concerts or other performances. In some of the larger cities in the United States, parades are organized. These parades show Jewish solidarity with Israel. Participants include members of synagogues, Jewish day schools, and Hebrew school classes, as well as all sorts of Jewish associations and groups.

For Jews, even those who have never visited Israel and never plan to go, the existence of their own independent state is a constant reassurance that they will be protected. As long as Israel survives, there will always be a place where Jews can go if they are threatened or persecuted and where Judaism can be practiced freely and unselfconsciously.

NOTES

1. David J. Wolpe, *Why Be Jewish* (New York: Henry Holt and Co., 1995), p. 74.

2. Paysach J. Krohn, *Bris Milah* (New York: Mesorah Publications, 1984) enumerates all the blessings necessary during the ceremony and the reasons behind them.

3. Ronald H. Isaacs, *Rites of Passage: A Guide to the Jewish Life Cycle* (New Jersey: K'tav, 1992), pp. 52–56.

4. Isaacs, *Rites of Passage*, p. 63–64.

5. *Encyclopaedia Judaica* (1st ed.), s.v. "Bar Mitzvah, Bat Mitzvah."

6. Ibid.

7. Ira Eisenstein, *Reconstructing Judaism: An Autobiography* (New York: Reconstructionist Press, 1986), p. 96.

8. Anita Diamant, *The New Jewish Wedding* (New York: Summit Books, 1985).

9. Philip and Hanna Goodman, *The Jewish Marriage Anthology* (Philadelphia: Jewish Publication Society, 1965), p. 27, citing Kiddushim 29b-30a.

10. Diament, *The New Jewish Wedding*, p. 190. This book gives excellent descriptions of many different marriage customs.

11. Emily Taitz, Sondra Henry, Cheryl Tallan, *The JPS Guide to Jewish Women: 600 B.C.E.–1900 C.E.* (Philadelphia: Jewish Publication Society, 2003), p. 40.

12. Maurice Lamm, *The Jewish Way in Death and Mourning* (New York: Jonathan David Publishers, 1969), p. 16.

13. Ibid., p. 67.

14. Theodore H. Gaster, *Festivals of the Jewish Year* (New York: William Sloane Assoc., 1952; 4th printing, 1968), pp. 267–268.

15. This song can be found in most siddurim (prayer books). In *Siddur Sim Shalom* the translation is on p. 263.

16. Gaster, *Festivals of the Jewish Year*, p. 122.

17. Ibid., p. 134.

18. Ibid., pp. 51–58.

19. Lag is actually the Hebrew letters that, in their numerical value, add to 33. The Hebrew letter lamed is 30 and the Hebrew letter gimel is three.

20. *Encyclopaedia Judaica*, s.v. "Shavuot."

21. Ibid. s.v. "Purims, special."

22. *Maccabees* I is considered the most historically accurate. Josephus' book, *The Jewish Wars,* is also an important source for the Maccabean uprising as is the Greek historian Polybius (*ca.* 204–122 B.C.E.).

23. Gaster, *Festivals of the Jewish Year,* p. 244.

24. *Encyclopaedia Judaica,* s.v. *"Simhat Torah"*; but see Gaster, *Festivals of the Jewish Year,* p. 99 who believes it originated in Western Europe.

25. Some Orthodox synagogues allow women to carry the Torah and make circuits in their own section, without mixing with men. Also, Orthodox women in women's minyans or prayer groups have all-women celebrations.

26. Mishnah Ta'anit 4:6 lists several others as well.

27. *Encyclopaedia Judaica,* s.v. "Av, the Ninth of: In Modern Israel."

28. Gaster, *Festivals of the Jewish Year,* p. 255.

6

MAJOR FIGURES

Some of the major personalities and leaders of the Jewish people are high-lighted here. There have been many great men and women during the more than 5,000 years of Jewish history, so these biographies are a small sample. Their lives are briefly outlined, along with some of the historical events that occurred during their times, so that the reader can better understand the significance of each one.

King David (10th–9th century B.C.E.)

David was the most beloved and successful of all the kings of Israel. According to the biblical account found in II Samuel, David bravely van-quished his enemies, then united the kingdom and expanded its borders, establishing Jerusalem as the capital. An alternative name for Jerusalem is still "The City of David."

The deeds of the great King David (1000–961 B.C.E.), such as the legend that in his youth he slew the mighty giant Goliath, have made him an im-portant and beloved figure in the history of the nation of Israel.[1] According to Jewish belief, no ruler was legitimate unless he was a descendant of David, and the Messiah himself was to come from the Davidic line. A popular folk song, sung by Jews in synagogues and in Zionist groups until today, proclaims: "David, the King of Israel, lives forever."

Like all kings of that period, David had multiple wives and concubines and numerous children. The one who inherited the kingship was Solomon, son of David and Bathsheba. It was Solomon who consolidated his father's victories and built the Holy Temple in Jerusalem. He ruled from 961–922 B.C.E. and was known to be a wise king, but he never proved his prowess in battle. His skills were more in the area of diplomacy.

Nehemiah (4th century B.C.E.)

Nehemiah, cupbearer (a personal attendant of high status) to the King of Persia, was one of the most important figures among the Israelites during the post-exilic period. He lived almost 100 years after the great Babylonian Empire had fallen to the Persians (538 B.C.E.). At that time, the new Persian King, Cyrus, gave permission for the Israelites to return to their homeland. A small number of Jews did return and rebuilt the Temple, but with no strong leader, they encountered serious problems, including opposition from factions of Jews who had remained in the land of Israel after the exile. Progress in restoring the city and organizing the inhabitants was at a standstill until the arrival of Nehemiah.

With the permission of the King, Nehemiah went to Jerusalem in approximately 440 B.C.E. and took charge. As administrator of the province that included the land of Judah and its capital city, Jerusalem, Nehemiah levied a tax on all the Jews of the land. His most important success was the rebuilding of the walls around Jerusalem and the protection of the city. This was a difficult challenge because of constant attacks by neighboring tribes. Nehemiah thus made Jerusalem and its surroundings safe for the inhabitants, preparing the way for Ezra, who then established the beginnings of what eventually developed into contemporary Jewish practice.

Ezra the Scribe (4th century B.C.E.)

Ezra was a Babylonian Jew who traveled to the land of Israel some time after Nehemiah's arrival, when the Temple had already been rebuilt. His official title was "scholar in the law of the God of Heaven" (Ezra 7:12), a title roughly equivalent to Minister of State for Jewish Affairs.[2] As a Kohen (priest), he had been disturbed by reports of the laxity of the people in following the proper rituals, and he immediately set out to reinstate the commandments (mitzvot).

One of Ezra's first acts was to read the Law of Moses aloud to all the people assembled outside the Temple (Nehemiah 8:4–7). He prayed and wept, hoping to make the inhabitants realize that they had been acting against

God by turning away from God's law. Ezra's efforts apparently won the Jews over to his point of view, and they confessed that they had sinned by ignoring the law of their people as it was written in the Torah.

The next problem Ezra tackled was intermarriage. As soon as he arrived from Babylonia, he heard from the Temple priests about the shocking number of Jews who had "not separated themselves from the peoples of the land" (Ezra 9:1). This meant not only that they were worshipping the gods of other peoples, but that they had taken wives and husbands from outside the Jewish fold, causing the tradition of their ancestors to be neglected and forgotten. Ezra succeeded in convincing the Jewish population to voluntarily put aside their foreign wives and return to traditional observance.[3]

By accomplishing these things, Ezra managed to reconstitute the nation and the religion of Israel. Under his guidance, the people agreed not to marry non-Jews and to follow the laws of the Sabbath and the agricultural rules as laid out in the Hebrew Bible. It is generally believed that the regular reading of the Torah began with Ezra's first public teaching. He reorganized the nation on the basis of the law of Moses, not by imposing his authority, but by teaching the people and helping them to take on this covenant of their own free will (Nehemiah 10). By doing this, he gave the children of Israel a religious basis on which to build. This achievement proved invaluable after the nation was totally destroyed more than 400 years later.

Judah Maccabee (d. 164 B.C.E.)

Judah Maccabee is one of the great national heroes of Jewish history, a warrior who, against all odds, led the Jews to victory. From approximately 600 B.C.E., the land of Israel became successively part of the Babylonian Empire, the Persian Empire, and then the Greek Empire, its territory fought over by warring factions. During those long centuries, the Jews did manage to wrest their land from foreign conquerors twice. The first time, they were led by Judah Maccabee.

Judah's date of birth is not recorded, but he became known in 165 B.C.E. during the Jewish rebellion against the Syrian/Greeks. The son of Mattathias, Judah was the middle son, one of five brothers. The others, Simon, Eliezer, John, and Jonathan, joined him in the fight against the Greeks. Although they were all recognized as heroes in that war for religious freedom and independence, it was Judah, called "the Maccabee," who caught the popular imagination and is considered the hero of the Hanukkah story (see also Chapter 5). Even though most of his exploits may be legendary by now, historians generally agree that Judah was the chief tactician and leader during the war. He died on the battlefield a short time after leading his victorious troops into Jerusalem in 164 B.C.E.

When the war ended with a Jewish victory, first Jonathan and then Simon, the last surviving brother, became king and high priest of an independent state called Judea. The dynasty he founded, referred to as the Hasmonean dynasty, however, became increasingly corrupt with each succeeding generation.[4] The Romans finally took over Judea in 63 B.C.E., dashing any hope for continuing an independent Jewish state.

Rabbi Akiva (50–135 C.E.)

The life of Rabbi Akiva, one of the greatest of the early sages, has become legendary. Akiva was a totally unlettered man who, according to reports, learned the alphabet together with his son. Inspired by his wife, Rachel, he eventually became a respected scholar, known especially for his concern for the poor and his humility and modesty.

Rabbi Akiva was one of the sages referred to collectively as the *Tanna-im* (teachers), from an Aramaic word meaning "to hand down orally."[5] It is the teachings of the Tanna-im that make up the Mishnah, an interpretation of the laws of the Bible, and much of what is known of this scholar is from the Mishnah itself.

Rabbi Akiva died a martyr's death. He was imprisoned, tortured, and executed by the Romans for openly teaching the Torah in defiance of a Roman edict forbidding it.

Simon Bar Kokhba (d. 135 C.E.)

Simon, another great national hero, followed in the footsteps of Judah Maccabee. He lived in the early decades of the second century, during the reign of the Emperor Hadrian (117–138 C.E.). Originally named Simon bar Kosibah, he was a strong and charismatic young man who claimed that he could reestablish a Jewish state. Many Jews, including the great Rabbi Akiva, believed in him, even claiming that he was the long-awaited Messiah. Because of this, they changed his name to Bar Kokhba, "son of a star." This alluded to the quotation from the Bible: "There shall step forth a star out of Jacob" (Numbers 24:17).

Simon Bar Kokhba did have some success. He organized and led a ferocious rebellion against the Romans that lasted for 3 1/2 years, from 132 to

135 C.E., eventually involving the entire Jewish population of the area. Bar Kokhba took the title of Nasi ("Prince") of Israel. Coins were minted with the inscription "Simon, Prince of Israel" and dated "Year one of the redemption of Israel." Simon was known as a harsh general and ruler, and his army, although greatly outnumbered, killed hundreds of Roman soldiers. In fact, the Roman general had to bring in additional forces to subdue this revolt.[6]

The uprising ended in 135 C.E. at the fortress of Betar in the Judean hills. Simon made his last stand there and died along with all his men. This defeat blotted out any hope that the Jews would regain their independence. Large sections of the population had been killed, deported, or sold into slavery. After the rebellion, the Romans initiated even harsher measures against the remaining Jews and their religious practices, and Emperor Hadrian had a pagan temple built in Jerusalem, now renamed Aelia Capitolina.

From the time of Simon's defeat, the major figures in Judaism were no longer kings, warriors, or high priests. The Jews turned to their laws, the one aspect of their nation that could not be destroyed. The scholars of Israel became their heroes and the centers of scholarship moved into the growing Diaspora.

Rabbi Meir and Beruriah (2nd century C.E.)

Rabbi Meir, a well-known and well-loved scholar, was one of Rabbi Akiva's disciples. Beruriah, Meir's wife, was also a prominent scholar. Because Beruriah was known as the only woman whose rulings were accepted as law, there are many stories about her throughout the Talmud. They present her as a wise teacher who often advised her husband concerning the law.

Meir, like Rabbi Akiva, was threatened by Roman officials and had to flee, but he was never caught. He later returned to the land of Israel where he became one of the officials of the Jews and a major contributor to the Mishnah.

Less is known of Beruriah's life and death. One legend claims that she killed herself after succumbing to a seducer, but this is from a medieval source and his been totally discredited. More recently, scholars have concluded that the many Talmudic stories about a wise women named Beruriah have been consolidated and actually involve several scholarly women, perhaps all with the same name. One was the wife of Rabbi Meir, one was the daughter of Rabbi Hananiah, and one has no known family.[7] Nevertheless, the single figure of Beruriah persists as one of the few recognized women scholars in Jewish history.

Judah the Prince (2nd–3rd century C.E.)

Judah, called "the Prince" (*haNasi*) and "our holy teacher," was the greatest of all the Tanna-im (scholars of the Mishnah) in the land of Israel. A descendant of the great Rabbi Hillel, Judah is credited with compiling and editing the six orders (volumes) of the Mishnah, a task that was completed in 200 C.E.

In addition to his scholarship, Judah was also a political leader and the Jewish people considered him a savior of Israel. Like his father, Rabban Simeon ben Gamliel, he was the Patriarch of Judea. He maintained excellent relations with the Roman emperors and, as a result, was able to improve the economic status of his people and teach them the Torah and the commandments. In general, he elevated the position of patriarch and he was respected and considered a spiritual and social leader of the nation.[8]

Rabbi Ashi (335–427/8 C.E.)

One of the most noted of the *Amora-im,* the sages who compiled the Talmud, was the Babylonian scholar, Ashi. Also known by his Aramaic title, Rabbana, Ashi was the head of the academy in Sura, Babylonia, for 60 years, from 371 C.E. During that time, he turned Sura into an influential and important center for Jewish learning and law and attracted many students.

Ashi was also a leader of his generation and his contemporaries likened him to Judah, *haNasi,* who lived in the land of Israel almost 200 years before him. He was held in high esteem by the Jewish community of Babylonia, from the Exilarch (the secular head of the Jewish community) down to the simple folk, and had an excellent relationship with the Persian rulers.

Together with his disciples, Ashi began the monumental work of editing the entire Talmud.[9] His work was completed by the next generation of Amora-im and then organized by the *Savora-im,* a group of later scholars. The Talmud was finally closed at the end of the 5th century, long after Ashi's death, but Ashi is recognized as the major figure in this endeavor.

Saadya (882–942 c.e.)

Over the course of 500 years, there were hundreds of *gaonim*, scholars who presided over the two major academies of Babylonia. Many were ordinary men, but a few were extraordinary. The one who stands above all these sages is Saadya, who was appointed *Gaon* of Sura in 928 c.e.

Saadya was born in Egypt, not in Babylonia, and because of this, his appointment to this high office broke precedent. However, he was a strong leader who had already made his mark on Jewish life by his stand against the Karaites (see also Chapter 3) and his insistence that the Babylonian, and not the Palestinian, sages should set the Jewish calendar.[10]

Gaon was a respected title in the Jewish world, and Saadya, like those before him who filled this role, had jurisdiction over the organization of the Jewish courts throughout Babylonia. They were considered the intellectual leaders of world Jewry and were allowed to issue decrees that were binding on all Jews. Questions concerning Jewish law were addressed to them from all parts of the world, and the gaonim would answer them according to the accepted practice in Babylonia. In this way, they united the Jews of the Diaspora, setting one general standard for all Jewish communities.

Besides making decisions on issues of Jewish law, Saadya made a major contribution to the Hebrew literature and philosophy of the period. He was strongly influenced by the Greek ideal of Reason and, in his principal work, *The Book of Doctrines and Beliefs,* he consolidated and harmonized the philosophy of reason with the Jewish faith.[11]

Saadya also revived the Sura academy itself and, although he was involved in some major conflicts within the Jewish community, he accomplished a great deal. Saadya was the first to integrate all the different beliefs and aspects of Judaism into one complete system.

After Saadya's death, Sherira Gaon and Hai Gaon were the most exceptional of his successors, but none ever reached the level of Saadya or accomplished as much. By the end of the 10th century, the cultural center of Babylonia was waning. Although the office of gaonate continued for two more centuries, the influence these leaders had once wielded in the Jewish world was on the decline and new centers of Jewish life were developing as the Jews moved farther West.

Rashi: Rabbi Shlomo Yitzhaki (1040–1105 C.E.)

Rabbi Solomon (Shlomo) ben Isaac (Yitzhaki) is best known by the acronym Rashi, from the first letters of his title and his names. Born in France in approximately 1040, Rashi lived at a time when the Jewish communities of northern Europe were beginning to grow and develop. He studied in Germany, where several respected academies were already functioning in the cities along the Rhine River. After many years of study, he returned to his native town of Troyes and set up his own school. In Troyes, Rashi became a scholar of renown, respected by Christians and Jews alike.

One of Rashi's first projects was a full commentary on all the books of the Hebrew Bible. Although he wrote his explanations in Hebrew, Rashi understood that many Jews, including scholars, no longer had a thorough knowledge of the Hebrew language. To help them, he wrote in clear and concise Hebrew, interspersed with words from the local language, to be sure that his meaning was clear. Instead of stressing complicated philosophical ideas in his comments, he concentrated on the plain sense of the stories and their meanings. This method made his writing accessible to even the least sophisticated students, and his work was used widely by both Jewish and Christian scholars of the Bible.

Rashi also wrote a full commentary on many of the books of the Talmud, using the same clear method he had used for his Bible commentary. This work was so widely accepted that all printed versions of the Talmud came to include Rashi's explanations.

Only a few details are known about Rabbi Shlomo's personal life. He was married and had three daughters, Yoheved, Miriam, and Rachel. Two of them married Rashi's students, and one of his sons-in-law, Rabbi Meir, and two of his grandsons, Samuel and Jacob, continued his work in France.[12] These sages became famous in their own right, but none ever accomplished as much as Rabbi Shlomo Yitzhaki, whose work is still being used today. Rashi's Bible commentary continues to be the first explanation of the Hebrew Bible to be studied by Jewish children throughout the world.

Rashi died in 1105, shortly after the First Crusade of 1096 and the murder and forced conversion of many European Jews by the Crusaders. In those last years of his life, he had to answer many legal questions concerning the converts and their Jewish relatives. One of his most famous rulings from this period is: "An Israelite, even though he has sinned, remains an Israelite."[13] In other words, Rashi explained, forced conversion does not make a Jew into a gentile, and his relatives must treat him or her according to Jewish law. This explanation was used often in succeeding generations, as Jews throughout Europe faced the choice of conversion or expulsion, conversion or death.

Maimonides: Rabbi Moshe ben Maimon (1135–1204 C.E.)

Considered to be the intellectual giant of Jewish history, Moses (Moshe) ben Maimon was also one of the most controversial. He was born in Cordova into a family of scholars who had lived in Spain for eight generations. When he was 13 years old, an invasion by the Berbers of North Africa forced the family to flee, and after many years of persecution and wandering, they settled in Egypt.

The years of instability seemed to have had little effect on Moses ben Maimon's intellectual life. Although he described the difficulties of a life of wandering in a letter, he continued studying both medicine and Jewish law, and even produced two short books.[14] At the age of 23, he began what would be one of his most important works, *Commentary on the Mishnah.* After that, he wrote *Book of the Commandments* and, after his arrival in Egypt, started work on his best-known book, *Mishneh Torah* (Repetition of the Torah).

The *Mishneh Torah,* sometimes called *Yad haHazakah* (The Strong Hand) is an extensive compendium of law. It took him a full 10 years to complete this work, which classified and codified all of Jewish law in an innovative way and combined it with Aristotle's philosophy of Reason. Within its pages are the 13 principles of the Jewish faith, some of which were considered extremely controversial at that time. Maimonides's claim that God was incorporeal, meaning that God was not a tangible Being, was considered shocking to many in that time. His theory that the age of the Messiah simply meant renewed political independence for the Jewish people was also contrary to the belief of many Jews.

As soon as the *Mishneh Torah* began to circulate, shortly after its completion in 1178, it met with opposition.[15] Many Jews in the East thought that it threatened the authority of the gaonim and of the Talmud itself. In the West, Jewish scholars saw a challenge in his stress on the principles of Reason and the ideas of the Greek philosopher Aristotle, fearing that they would cast doubt on traditional Jewish beliefs. These philosophical battles continued to surround Moses ben Maimon's work and brought him great fame during his lifetime and after his death.

Moses Maimonides (the Greek version of his name) was able to continue his scholarly activities in Cairo because his younger brother, David, a businessman and trader, supported him. When David drowned at sea, Maimonides was forced to earn a living. He turned to the practice of medicine but did not give up his studies.

In 1177, he was named head of the Jewish community of Fostat/Cairo. In response to queries sent to him, he wrote hundreds of responses explaining questions of Jewish law for individuals and communities. In 1185, his success in the practice of medicine led to an appointment as personal physician to the Vizier of Egypt in the court of Saladin I, and his fame as a physician spread. The last of his books, *Guide of the Perplexed,* was written in 1190.

Guide of the Perplexed is a philosophical work, addressed to those who are searching for faith and who see a conflict between faith and reason. Written in Arabic rather than Hebrew, it became one of Maimonides's most popular works and remains relevant in modern times.

The years from 1185 until his death in 1204 were Maimonides's busiest period. In a famous letter, written in 1199, he described the daily demands of his life, juggling his work as a doctor, as head of the Jewish community, and as an independent scholar.[16]

He wrote many personal letters during his lifetime and is the first Jew whose correspondence has been preserved. In contrast to his books, which are reasoned and unemotional, Moses ben Maimon's letters reveal a man who is emotional, humble, and compassionate. Respect for this great scholar continually grew, and he was referred to as "the light of east and west and unique master and marvel of the generation."[17]

Maimonides is also known as the *Rambam,* an acronym from the initials of Rabbi Moshe ben Maimon. Almost nothing is known of his wife, but he did have one son, Abraham, who was also a scholar. Abraham succeeded Moshe as head of the Jewish community of Cairo but never achieved his father's greatness.

Moses ben Maimon's works are well known today, and many of his rulings and opinions are still followed. He is considered "one of the most illustrious figures in Judaism in the post-Talmudic era and one of the greatest of all time."[18]

Gracia Nasi (1510–1569)

Gracia Nasi, originally named Beatrice de Luna, was born in Portugal as a crypto (secret)-Jew. After becoming a widow in 1536, Beatrice managed to leave Portugal and to turn her husband's trading business into a thriving international enterprise. She lived first in Antwerp, then Italy, and finally Istanbul, where she settled at the invitation of the sultan, ruler of the Ottoman Empire. Free at last to openly admit that she was a Jew, she adopted her Hebrew name, Hannah, which means "grace" and came to be known as Dona (Lady) Gracia. In Turkey, she also took the last name of Nasi (Prince).

Gracia Nasi was the most prominent Jewish philanthropist of the sixteenth century, contributing money for hospitals, schools, and synagogues throughout the Ottoman Empire. Even before moving to the safety of Turkey, she helped organize an underground railroad to help crypto-Jews escape the Inquisition.

One of Gracia's projects was the funding of a Jewish settlement in Tiberius, in the land of Israel, making her the first Jew to support resettlement in the ancient Jewish homeland. Gracia Nasi established the community in Tiberius with the help of her son-in-law, Joseph Nasi, and the full approval of the sultan. The settlement flourished for a short time, but it was neglected after her death in 1569.

Isaac Luria (1534–1572)

The philosophy and beliefs of Isaac Luria, nicknamed haAri (from the Hebrew initials for "The Divine Rabbi Isaac"), were, in many ways, a direct contrast to the idea of a rational faith as put forth by the earlier sages Saadya and Maimonides. Luria was born in Jerusalem, but after his father's death, he and his mother moved to Egypt and he was raised in the home of his maternal uncle.

Although he studied traditional religious subjects in Egypt, he became interested in the texts of Kabbalah, the mystical books of Judaism, at a young age. Sometime during the 1560s, Luria wrote his only book, a commentary on part of the Zohar, a principle text of the Kabbalists, but there is no hint in it of the innovative theory he would later develop.

Luria returned to the land of Israel in 1569 or 1570 and settled in Safed. It is here that he developed his elaborate mystical ideas, including the concept of *tikkun olam*, "repair of the world." According to this theory, in order for the Messiah to come, bringing with him the promise of the World to Come, Jews must first repair this world. They could do this by prayer, good deeds, following the commandments, and spiritual methods to attain closeness with God.[19]

Luria's ideas were passed on to his many disciples, who in turn transmitted them to others. His principle disciple, Hayyim Vital, was responsible for writing down and preserving many of his teacher's theories and making them known to a wider circle. Although not originally a part of mainstream Judaism, the concept of tikkun olam eventually became more accepted in the Jewish world. It justified the messianic movements that developed after Luria's death, inspired many European Jewish scholars, both men and women, and was included in the mystical philosophy of the Hasidic Movement of the eighteenth century.

The Ari died in Safed in 1572, much beloved and respected. His innovative and unique ideas strengthened the mystical and magical aspects of the Jewish religion. Long after his death, those ideas inspired many Jews who did not feel at home with the legalistic trend that was developing in Judaism. Today, tikkun olam has become a part of the Jewish vocabulary. Modern Jews use it as a metaphor for doing good works in the community.

Shabbetai Zevi (1626–1676)

Shabbetai Zevi was one of the most famous pretenders in Jewish history. A few other names of false messiahs do appear from time to time, but none was more popular than he.

Over the many centuries of exile and oppression, Jews longed for a Messiah, believing that his arrival would usher in a Golden Age of peace. When the Messiah came, they thought, Jews would finally be free in their own land and would no longer suffer persecution. Because this belief was so strong, it was perhaps inevitable that some individual leader would arise to capture the imagination of the Jews and convince them that he was indeed the Messiah. In the seventeenth century, that man was Shabbetai Zevi.

Shabbetai was born in Smyrna (now Izmir), Turkey, part of a middle-class family. He was well educated and had already developed an interest in Kabbalah during his adolescence. Shabbetai Zevi was both charismatic and unstable, experiencing long periods of depression and then of exaltation. He often committed bizarre acts that ran counter to traditional Jewish practice, such as publicly pronouncing the name of God, traditionally forbidden, or transgressing other laws. He began claiming that he was the Messiah.

Finally, his behavior led to his banishment from Smyrna in approximately 1651. Shebbetai took this opportunity to travel throughout the Middle East. Although the rabbis of Salonika also eventually banished him, he did make many friends and developed a small following. In Cairo, he married a woman from Poland named Sarah, "an Ashkenazi girl of doubtful reputation," with whom he had two children.[20]

His brief years of leadership began when he met Nathan of Gaza, a young mystic and rabbi who confirmed Shabbetai Zevi's own beliefs and publicly proclaimed him the Messiah in 1665. Great excitement spread throughout the Jewish communities and Shabbetai Zevi's following grew. He called for general repentance, promising that this would bring about the final redemption. He also sent out letters to all the communities of the Diaspora, urging them to accept him as the Messiah and naming Nathan of Gaza as his prophet.

Returning to his native city of Smyrna later in the year, he was met with suspicion, but the rabbis hesitated to bring charges against him because of his growing popularity. Everywhere Shabbetai Zevi traveled, he was met with respect and adulation, and his strange behavior was now explained as the result of his closeness to God. News about this new Messiah spread west into Europe and south into North Africa, and Jews throughout the world eagerly awaited the call to return to the land of Israel.

Finally, Turkish officials, suspicious of all this activity, arrested Shabbetai Zevi in 1666 and gave him a choice: convert to Islam or die. Shabbetai Zevi chose conversion, causing shock and disbelief among most of his followers. Some were so convinced that he was the true Messiah, however, that they followed him into Islam, trusting a higher purpose in this decision. Other Jews accepted the disappointment and returned to their everyday lives. A small group continued to believe that Shabbetai Zevi was the Messiah in spite of all evidence to the contrary. They formed a secret sect, the Doenmeh, developing traditions based on his erratic practices.

The now-converted false Messiah continued to live in Turkey, practicing the Muslim religion along with Judaism, and explaining the Kabbalah to his loyal followers. The rabbis forbade any mention of his practices and ignored his teachings.

Ten years after his conversion, in 1676, Shabbetai Zevi died. But such was the power of his personality and his strange ideas that the Shabbatian Movement persisted for more than a century after his death. It influenced the practice of Judaism, especially in Poland, Italy, and Turkey, and traces of it are still being uncovered in the literature of the period.

Shabbetai Zevi was not the first Jew to claim he was the Messiah, but he was the last. By the eighteenth century, the idea of a tangible Messiah had been generally discredited and became, for many Jews, simply a symbol of better times to come.

The Baal Shem Tov: Israel ben Eliezer (1700–1760)

Hasidism began in the mid-1700s, in southern Poland, because of one charismatic man named Israel ben Eliezer (see also Chapter 3). Israel, born in 1700, became known as The *Baal Shem Tov* ("Master of the Divine Name"), a title commonly given to mystics who invoked the secret names of God for magical and curative purposes.

Little is known of Israel's early life except that he was orphaned at a young age and brought up by the Jewish community of Okup, Podolia. Although given a good education, he preferred other activities to studying the law. He worked as a teacher's aid and sang songs and told stories to the children. Although he himself was learned, he felt a close tie with less educated people, and he took it upon himself to teach them the way to God with parables and by example. He often roamed the woods to commune privately with God and was known as a miracle worker.

The Baal Shem Tov left no writings of his own, but he gradually attracted a following of Jews. His disciples were inspired by his belief that closeness to God came through love, devotion, and sincere prayer. He preached against the study of the law for purposes of self-perfection. Instead, he advised scholars to reach out to the common people and help to raise them to a higher level of holiness. He also discouraged Jews from practicing asceticism, depriving themselves of personal comforts in order to become more holy. Instead, he taught Jews to worship God with joy and to take pleasure in life, to focus on "the inner light which is immanent in the action."[21]

The Baal Shem Tov married and had a son, Zevi, and a daughter, Edel. His son was shy and retiring and was not able to succeed his father as a leader, but Edel was very close to her father. She learned his methods of mystical healing and was revered as a holy woman. Edel married one of the Baal Shem Tov's students and had two sons and a daughter named Feige. Feige's son, Nahman, became a leader among the Hasidim. He is still famous today and is known as Rabbi Nahman of Bratislav.[22]

Israel ben Eliezer Baal Shem Tov died in 1760, but his disciples kept his ideas alive and formed their own congregations and communities throughout Poland and Russia, each with its own *tzaddik* ("righteous one") as spiritual leader. Over the years, the philosophy of Hasidism changed and began to stress more intellectual pursuits, but the Baal Shem Tov's teachings permeated all of Judaism and turned mysticism from a marginal study by a few learned men into a popular movement.

Elijah Gaon of Vilna (1720–1797)

Elijah ben Solomon Zalman, a brilliant scholar, was born in a small town in Lithuania. From his earliest years he showed strong intellectual talents, and as a young man, was granted a stipend by a learned relative so that he could spend his days studying. After his marriage, he settled in Vilna and was given an additional stipend by the Jewish community of that city, even though he held no communal office. This was a reflection not only of Elijah's genius, but also of the belief that those who studied Jewish texts were of great benefit to the Jewish community. In recognition of his scholarship, Elijah was given the honorary title of gaon and was often referred to only as "the Vilna Gaon."

Elijah did not limit his studies to Jewish law. He expanded his interests to secular subjects, especially astronomy, geometry, algebra, and geography, explaining that these disciplines helped him to understand the Torah and the Talmud. He encouraged the translation into Hebrew of many modern scientific works but disapproved of philosophy and especially frowned on the Enlightenment ideas that were already spreading east from Germany by the late 1700s.

Although the Vilna Gaon was a retiring, almost reclusive person, he was much sought out for his advice on communal affairs and for his teachings. He believed in the "eternity of the Torah," explaining that "everything that was, is and will be is included in the Torah."[23] Therefore, nothing could be changed or omitted; even the smallest alteration in Jewish legal writing was unacceptable, as it detracted from the entirety of the law.

This commitment to every detail of the law may have been what caused Elijah's violent opposition to the new Hasidic Movement that began to spread after the death of the Baal Shem Tov. The Vilna Gaon became the leader of those who sought to eliminate the new movement completely, even approving of the burning of Hasidic books and the excommunication of their leaders. He feared that the new teachings of the Hasidim cast aspersions on the importance of Torah and would cause a major rift in the community.

During his lifetime, Elijah Gaon wrote many books, both on Jewish subjects and on secular science. Besides numerous commentaries on the Bible and the Mishnah, he wrote on mathematics and astronomy, and was interested in music as well. He disapproved of the tendency among Jewish scholars of his time to ignore secular learning and warned that it cast aspersions on Israel's name among the nations.

The Vilna Gaon died in 1797, and his personality was later overshadowed by the more colorful leaders of the Hasidic Movement that he had worked so hard to eliminate. However, his ideas persisted among most mainstream Jews. They continued his commitment to preserving the law in its entirety and built on his teachings to form the Orthodox Movement of the nineteenth century (see also Chapter 3).

Moses Mendelssohn (1729–1786)

One of the giants of the eighteenth century, Moses Mendelssohn represented a point of view that was considered the greatest threat of all by traditional Jews like Elijah Gaon and the Baal Shem Tov. Although always an observant Jew who followed the law in its entirety, Mendelssohn was among the first Jews of his time to embrace the modern ideas of the Enlightenment.

Born in Dessau, Germany, the young Moses showed an early aptitude for learning. At the age of 14, he followed his teacher to Berlin and established himself there. After years of poverty and study, he eventually found work as a bookkeeper. He married and had two sons and two daughters.

In Berlin, the capital and cultural center of Prussia, Mendelssohn quickly expanded his interests. Instead of limiting himself to works in the Hebrew language and in Yiddish, the spoken language of most of Eastern Europe's Jews, he learned German and began writing in that language. This brought him into the world of German culture and literature, and he gained fame among Christian philosophers and thinkers. Eventually he became known as "the German Socrates."[24]

Mendelssohn firmly believed that it was possible to be an observant Jew and also participate fully in the life and culture of the state in which one lives. He wrote several essays and books discussing this concept, and his ideas won a great deal of respect from his contemporaries. He had close Christian friends who agreed with his theory of freedom of conscience and supported his advice to Jews. "Adapt yourself to the morals and the constitution of the land to which you have been removed," Mendelssohn urged Jews, "but hold fast to the religion of your fathers, too. Bear both burdens as well as you can."[25]

Mendelssohn was certainly not the first Jewish philosopher to urge loyalty to an adopted homeland. Samuel, one of the great sages of the Talmud, had declared "the law of the land is the law" and this was a standard for Jews everywhere.[26] Nor was Mendelssohn the only Jew who had tried to combine faith and reason. He was following in the footsteps of such earlier giants as Saadya Gaon and Moses Maimonides. But in Mendelssohn's time, reason had become the ultimate guide for Christian culture and thus even more important for Jews if they wanted to enter the modern world. Not content with merely a discussion of Greek philosophy, Mendelssohn actually studied the arguments and the language of Socrates and used the style of this ancient Greek philosopher to prove his own points.[27]

Philosophy was not Mendelssohn's only interest, however. Using the prestige he gained among his influential Christian friends, he urged the governments of the various German states to emancipate the Jews and give them equal rights. He became the principal Jew in Europe, and other Jews naturally turned to him to help in the fight against prejudice. In Mendelssohn's time, Jews were still forced to live in ghettos, prevented from working in all professions and from living where they chose or serving in public office.

Mendelssohn wrote many books, both in Hebrew and in German. Among his most important and influential work was his German translation of the Hebrew Bible. The first book, Genesis, was completed in 1780 and others followed quickly. This first German edition had an enormous impact on the Jews, not only in Germany but in many other countries where German was spoken. Completed in 1783, it "caused a cultural revolution among German Jews."[28]

Another of his books, *Jerusalem, or Religious Power and Judaism,* challenged the government itself. Insisting on the separation of Church and State, he explained that Jews could not hope to gain citizenship in a Christian state, nor could anyone expect to be able to exercise freedom of conscience in such a state. This idea was well before its time, and Mendelssohn painstakingly laid out the logic. The state, he asserted, governed the relations between humans while the Church watched over a human's relationship to God.

In the second part of the book, he addressed the Jewish faith itself, insisting that it was a rational faith. Mendelssohn claimed that the only thing that distinguished Jew from non-Jew was not religion. The difference lay in the distinctive laws and commandments given to the Jews at Mt. Sinai.

There was much opposition to Mendelssohn's philosophy. Some said that it denied Judaism's characteristics as a nation and made it just another religion. Others were critical of his efforts because they drew Jews away from Talmudic studies and encouraged them to become interested in European secular culture.[29]

Jews have long since repudiated Mendelssohn's definition of Judaism and its ultimate meaning. Even his own children found it impossible to follow his example, and three of the four ultimately converted to Christianity. Nevertheless, he made an impression on Judaism that was not easily ignored.

Moses Mendelssohn was the first Jewish philosopher to address the conflict facing many Jews: how to reconcile the values of Judaism and the values of the modern world. After Mendelssohn's death, different Jews came up with a number of different answers.

Moses (1784–1885) and Judith (1784–1862) Montefiore

Moses and Judith Montefiore were English Jews and philanthropists who supported many projects throughout the world and helped advance Jewish settlement in Israel. Born in 1784, Moses was from an old Italian-Jewish family that had moved to England in the early eighteenth century and had settled in London. He was licensed as one of only 12 Jewish brokers and eventually achieved success as a banker. Working with Nathan Meyer Rothschild, his wife's sister's husband, he became one of the richest Jews in England.

Judith Cohen Montefiore, from Ashkenazi roots, was born in England the same year as her husband. She and Moses were married in 1812. They had no children, and she was able to work together with her husband in support of Jewish and non-Jewish causes.

In 1827, the Montefiores made the first of seven visits to the land of Israel, then called Palestine. Appalled at the poverty they found, they determined to help the Jews there end their dependence on charity. One of the Montefiores' projects, an agricultural colony outside the walls of the old city of Jerusalem, still exists today. It is called, in his honor, Yemin Moshe.

The Montefiores were among the most famous Jews in nineteenth-century England. Moses was politically active and fought for civil rights for Jews. Knighted by the English Crown in 1837, he was one of the few Jews to be so honored. Nine years later, in 1846, he was given the title of baron in recognition of his humanitarian efforts on behalf of world Jewry.

Because of the respect in which Montefiore was held, he was often asked to serve as an unofficial emissary whenever a crisis occurred in any Jewish community in the world. In 1840, Montefiore was called to mediate with the Syrian government in an infamous blood libel charge. The blood libel, the belief that Jews killed Christians to obtain their blood for secret Jewish rituals, had been known in the Middle Ages but had disappeared, for the most part, during the Enlightenment. Its reappearance in the nineteenth century was a great shock, especially in the West, as it became known that members of the ancient Syrian-Jewish community had been arrested and tortured. "The Damascus Affair" became world famous, and Montefiore's part in gaining the release of those Jewish prisoners who were still alive won him world renown as a Jewish statesman.[30] His wife had accompanied him on this mission and Moses publicly claimed: "I owe her a debt of gratitude" for her counsel.[31]

In 1846, he visited Russia in an attempt to help alleviate Jewish persecution there. Then in 1850, Montefiore was again called in to help, this time in the Mortara case. This was a case of a Jewish child in Sardinia (Italy) who was converted by his nursemaid and then abducted by the Catholic Church. Although Montefiore did not succeed in reversing the outcome here, his attempts added to his prestige and he was called to many other missions abroad.

In addition to helping her husband, Lady Montefiore was also devoted to her own causes. She was an officer of the Jews' Orphan Asylum and a patron of the Jewish Ladies' Loan and Visiting Society, and she funded programs to educate girls in cooking and homemaking. She is credited with writing the first Anglo-Jewish cookbook to be published in England.

Judith Cohen Montefiore died in 1862, right after celebrating her fiftieth anniversary. Moses, grief-stricken at her death, established a college as a memorial to her. It was called the Judith Lady Montefiore College at Ramsgate. In his eulogy, he acknowledged his indebtedness to his wife "whose enthusiasm for everything that is noble, and whose religiousness sustained me in my career."[32]

Moses Montefiore died in 1885 at the age of 101 years. His 100th birthday was celebrated as a public holiday by the Jews in England and all over the world.

Theodore Herzl (1860–1904)

Theodore Herzl, one of the most important figures in the Zionist Movement, is considered the father of the modern state of Israel. Yet he began life as an assimilated Jew who knew little about Judaism. He devoted himself to secular culture and to his own career as a writer.

Theodore Herzl is considered the father of
modern Israel, even though he died long before the state was ever established and never
lived there. Courtesy of Central Zionist Archives, Jerusalem, Israel.

Herzl was born in Budapest, Hungary, into a prosperous Jewish family.
He was given both a secular and a religious education but showed little
interest in Jewish affairs. At his parents' suggestion, he studied law but his
interest was in literature. He traveled and worked as a playwright and jour-
nalist for many years, writing in German. But in 1891, he was offered the
job of Paris correspondent for the *Neue Freie Press*, an important, German-
language newspaper, and his life quickly changed.

As soon as he took up his new post, Herzl became involved in world affairs and was in a unique position to witness the growing antisemitism that
was spreading across Europe. His reporting of the Dreyfus case became the
catalyst that would radically change his point of view.

Alfred Dreyfus was a Jewish officer in the French Army who was wrongly
accused of treason in 1894, found guilty, and given a life sentence. Herzl
might not have paid much attention to this verdict except for the mobs that
stood outside the courthouse crying, "Death to the Jews!" As Herzl wrote
in his diary: If such things could happen "in republican, modern, civilized
France, a century after the Declaration of Human Rights," then there was
no hope that Jews could be safe in Europe.[33]

From that realization came plans to establish a Jewish state, where Jews would be safe from antisemitism and free to develop normally. His first step was to write a pamphlet presenting his ideas to the public. Called *Der Judenstadt* ("The Jewish state"), it was published in February 1896 with little fanfare and did not immediately garner a large following. Most prosperous Jews regarded it as a fantasy, and those already committed to the Zionist idea saw it as nothing new.

In fact, it was not new, and Herzl himself was the first to admit it. However, Herzl did bring something new to this old idea: a tremendous amount of commitment and energy, and a willingness to try anything to achieve his goal. The saying "If you will it, it is no dream," attributed to Herzl, may not have been an exact quotation, but his actions embodied that principle.

After the publication of *Der Judenstadt*, Herzl immediately conceived of a plan to involve world leaders. He tried to obtain an audience with the Ottoman (Turkish) Sultan and convince him to allow Jews to settle on a small part of his land, the part referred to as Palestine. In return, he promised that Jewish bankers would help him pay off his huge debt. Herzl also spoke with officials in Germany, Russia, England, and France, trying to enlist their support for a Jewish state. Although he had little success and was often discouraged, he never gave up, insisting that the old method of slow settlement would not work. What was needed, he said, was legal recognition from the nations of the world.

Another aspect of Herzl's plan was to convince Jewish philanthropists to contribute money to his project. He first approached German philanthropist Baron de Hirsch, who flatly refused to consider it. Later, he met with the heads of all the Rothschilds, a large, philanthropic family. They also dismissed his ideas as unworkable. Even though Baron Edmond de Rothschild of France had already been giving aid to Jewish farming settlements in the land of Israel, he felt that a Jewish state was inconceivable and would not back Herzl.

Herzl's third thrust was to interest the Jewish people in his scheme. He did this almost single-handedly, first by establishing a Zionist newspaper, *Die Welt* ("The World"), and then by organizing a Zionist Congress. And this is where he had his greatest success. The first Congress, held in Basel, Switzerland, in 1897, included Jews from all over Europe and America, representing a variety of points of view and many different associations and groups.

From this first Congress, considered a milestone in Jewish history, the Zionist Movement grew steadily. Other Congresses followed, and, in between, Herzl continued his diplomatic activities, enlisting the aid of government officials to obtain an audience with the sultan.

The sultan finally did receive him in 1899, but Herzl was not able to convince him that his scheme was workable. When Turkey introduced new restrictions on Jewish immigration, it was a severe blow to Herzl and to the Zionist Movement.

After this failure, Herzl turned to negotiations with Germany and England, but these, too, were inconclusive. With the new Zionist organization in turmoil, and little to show for all his efforts, crises arose one after the other. Some Zionists, despairing of a Jewish state in their old homeland, were ready to settle for another location. Argentina was suggested, along with Uganda, and a section of Egypt, then controlled by the British, but all were violently opposed by most Jews at the Congress. Then in 1903, there was a pogrom (an organized attack on Jews) in Kishinev, Russia. This was quickly followed by the Russian government's ban on collections for the new Jewish National Fund.[34]

In 1904, one year after the Kishinev pogrom, Theodore Herzl died from heart disease and pneumonia. He was 44 years old. Even though none of his goals had yet been achieved, he never gave up hope, ordering that he should be buried in Vienna, but only until there was a Jewish state in Palestine.

Forty-five more years would pass and two world wars would occur before the nations of the world, stunned by the near-destruction of Europe's Jews in the Nazi Holocaust, would agree to recognize a Jewish state. In 1949, one year after his dream became a reality, Herzl's remains were brought to Israel. He is buried on a mountain in Jerusalem named Mount Herzl, in his honor.

Abraham Isaac Kook (1865–1935)

Abraham Isaac Kook, the first chief rabbi of Israel, was born in Latvia. He received a traditional Jewish education but soon branched out to other disciplines. Early in his career he made aliyah (ascended to the land of Israel) and became a rabbi in Jaffa. In his time, this was a shocking and even rebellious decision, as most Orthodox rabbis believed that Jews must wait for the Messiah to come before they could return to the ancient Jewish homeland.

In spite of opposition, Kook remained steadfast in his commitment to the Zionist ideal, urging European Jews to come and settle on the land. Eventually, Kook was appointed first Ashkenazi Chief Rabbi of Israel, a post that was created in 1921, even before the establishment of an independent state.

A prolific writer, Kook wrote many books explaining his theories on religion and secular life, insisting that the two must be combined. He urged religious Jews to develop a passion for justice and not ignore the betterment of the world. At the same time, he urged those who fought for justice not to turn their backs on religion. He refused to separate the sacred from the profane, insisting that "together [they] influence the spirit of man."[35]

During his time as Chief Rabbi, Kook was the conscience of the Jews of the land of Israel, challenging them to accept the Torah in their lives and "do what is right and good in the sight of the Lord" (Deuteronomy 6:18). To him, this meant curtailing the excesses of capitalism and striving toward a greater morality.

At Kook's death in 1935, the world was on the verge of a major war and Israel was not yet recognized as an independent state. But Kook was convinced that the Balfour Declaration of 1917, promising a homeland for the Jews, had ushered in a new era of renewal for the Jewish people and that statehood was inevitable. He was mourned as a great teacher and mystic and a great humanitarian.

Chaim Weizmann (1874–1952)

When the new state of Israel was established in 1948, Chaim Weizmann was named President. This was largely an honorific post, but one he had earned by his commitment to Zionism over the years. Weizmann was born in 1874 in White Russia, the third in a family of 15 children. He attended a technical school and then a university in Germany and came into contact with the young Zionists who were studying in Berlin. After reading Theodore Herzl's book, *Der Judenstadt*, he attended the first Zionist Congress and began a growing commitment to the cause.

Weizmann ultimately settled in England, where, he believed, there was the least antisemitism, and obtained a post in chemistry at Manchester University. It was in England that he had the opportunity to help the Allied cause in World War I by his invention of artificial acetone, a product necessary for the production of high explosives. During those years, he also met some of the important officials of the British government and was able to speak with them about the need for a Jewish homeland. These talks proved to be an important factor when Turkey lost its territories in the Middle East as a result of the War.

Chaim Weizmann, a well-known scientist, was chosen as the first President of the modern state of Israel. Courtesy of Central Zionist Archives, Jerusalem, Israel.

One of Weizmann's early contacts was Lord Balfour. Balfour was the Foreign Minister of England who was responsible for issuing the Balfour Declaration in 1917, officially favoring the development of a Jewish homeland in Palestine. Weizmann later persuaded the British to allow him to travel to Palestine as the head of a small commission and take the first steps to implement the Declaration. While there, he laid the cornerstone of the first Hebrew University in Jerusalem and visited the Emir Faisal, commander of the Arab revolt. His goal was to try to gain the good will of the Arabs. Although Weizmann did succeed in establishing some friendly terms with Faisal, in the long run, Arab enmity toward a Jewish state was implacable and continues to this day.[36]

Weizmann's Zionist commitment continued unabated through the years of the British Mandate and he took a leadership role with the continuing Zionist Congress. He was elected President of the World Zionist Organization in 1921, but, by then, his influence with the leaders in the British government was waning. Most of his friends were no longer in power, and those who were did not feel any obligation to him or his cause. His offer to work for free, helping the British in the development of synthetic rubber during World War II, did not move them to be sympathetic. As World War II raged, England kept the borders of Palestine closed to Jewish immigration.

After the War, Weizmann traveled once again to Palestine, to celebrate his 70th birthday. In his honor, an Institute for Science was founded in the city of Rehovot. Called the Weizmann Institute, it was and remains a renowned center of research. But Weizmann was not ready to settle in the land of Israel. He continued to travel in the cause of Zionism, meeting with Jewish and gentile leaders in the United States and England, desperately trying to sway them to look favorably on an independent Jewish state.

When the Jewish state was finally established, Weizmann was 73 years old. As the first President of Israel, he served with the first Prime Minister, David ben Gurion. His official residence, in Rehovot, was close to the Institute where he had his own laboratory, but he continued traveling, now as President, on official visits to other nations. His first such visit was to Washington, D.C., at the invitation of President Harry S. Truman.

Weizmann died in 1952. Although not all Jews viewed him sympathetically, he is generally accepted as one who helped the most to lay the political foundations of the state of Israel.

David Ben Gurion (1886–1973)

David Ben Gurion, the first prime minister of a modern Jewish state, is recognized as one of the original builders of the state of Israel. He was born in Russian Poland, in 1886, into a family of confirmed Zionists and settled in Palestine in 1906, working in the orange groves and wineries already established by earlier Jewish settlers. He quickly became a leader among the young Zionists and urged others to make aliyah to the land of Israel. The word aliyah, the Hebrew word referring to immigration to Israel, means "ascent." It is a reflection of the philosophical idea that for a Jew, living in Israel is more praiseworthy than living in any other land. Ben Gurion firmly believed that every Jew should "come up" to Israel.

Ben Gurion was also committed to socialism, and he helped to establish and lead many of the workers' organizations in pre-state Israel that still exist today.

After World War I, Palestine was taken from Turkey and given to England as a mandate, and the British government began to restrict Jewish immigration into that region. Ben Gurion immediately condemned the policy, referred to as "the White Paper." While actively defying these poli-

David Ben Gurion was elected the first prime
minister of Israel and led the country for
many years. Courtesy of Central Zionist Archives, Jerusalem, Israel.

cies and working to help illegal immigrants who were escaping from persecution in Europe, he nevertheless gave unconditional support to England
during World War II. Immediately after that war, he again urged Jews to
settle in the emerging Jewish state and formulated a new political program
for the Zionist Movement.

When the United Nations finally voted for Jewish statehood, and an independent state was declared on May 14, 1948, Ben Gurion became the
provisional head of government. One year later, he was elected to the post
of prime minister, a position he held until his retirement in 1953. He was
later called back to serve as defense minister under the second prime minister, Moshe Sharett, and in 1955 was again chosen as prime minister. He
served the government of Israel until 1965, when, amidst continuing political controversy, he lost the support of his party.

Ben Gurion died in 1973. He had presided over the early organization of
the Jewish state of Israel, had helped create its basic form of government,
established many of its institutions, helped to build its army, and presided
over its development into a viable, democratic nation.

Since Ben Gurion's death, many others have served as prime minister of the state of Israel. Among them, Golda Meir, Menachem Begin, and Yitzhak Rabin stand out as important leaders, attempting to both defend their country and to put an end to continual war and hostility from its neighbors. Those who rule Israel today are still to be judged by history.

Martin Buber (1878–1965)

One of the great Jewish philosophers of modern times, Martin Buber was born into a Viennese Jewish family of renowned scholars. He began the traditional learning of Jewish law at an early age but quickly became interested in other subjects and studied in several universities in Germany. He joined the Zionist Movement in 1902, and in 1903, while at the University of Berlin, he was appointed editor of *Die Welt,* the Zionist newspaper that had been founded by Theodore Herzl. At this time, he also turned to a complete study of Hasidism, a topic to which he devoted five years. During that time he wrote several books on the practices and legends of the Hasidim, including *Tales of Rabbi Nahman, The Legends of the Baal Shem*, and *Hasidism and the Modern Man*. He also founded a Jewish monthly magazine, *Der Jude*, a publication that reflected the ideas of the Jewish renaissance movement in Central Europe.

Buber is best known for the unique philosophy of dialogue that he developed. He divided human relationships into two kinds: the "I—it" relationship, typical of relationships between humans and material things, and the "I—Thou" relationship. The second of these two is the more valuable. It is a real dialogue between equals, characterized by directness, mutuality, and openness. Such relationships, Buber explained, are the ideal and the model for a true relationship with God who is "the Eternal Thou." His book, *I and Thou,* is devoted to a full exposition of his theory. It was first published in 1923 but remains a well-known and respected philosophical work and has had much influence on Christian theology.[37]

From 1925, Buber taught Jewish religion and philosophy at the University of Frankfurt, Germany. He remained there until 1938 when, along with so many other Jews, he was forced to flee and took up residence in Jerusalem. He was appointed Professor of Social Philosophy at the Hebrew University and, after World War II, was invited to speak in many countries. He lectured and taught in the United States in 1951 and 1952.

One of Buber's interests was improving understanding between Israeli Jews and Arabs. This effort was the basis of his concept of Hebrew Human-

Martin Buber. Courtesy of the Library of the
Jewish Theological Seminary.

ism, first put forward at the Zionist Congress of 1921. In Israel, he became
a leader of *Ihud,* an organization that aimed at a bi-national state of Arabs
and Jews, but this plan was never accepted by a majority of either Jews or
Arabs.

Buber, the recipient of many international awards and honors, died in
Israel in 1965. He was recognized as one of the spiritual leaders of his generation.

Menachem Mendel Schneerson: The Lubavitcher Rebbe
(1902–1993)

Menachem Mendel Schneerson, revered as The Lubavitcher Rebbe, was
born at the very beginning of the twentieth century, in southern Ukraine.
He was the descendant of a scholarly family, founders of the Habad movement of Hasidism, and he himself was considered a Torah prodigy. After
mastering many of the skills of the Jewish curriculum, he studied math
and science at the University of Berlin. In 1933, after Adolf Hitler came to

power and Jews were banned from German schools and universities, he moved to Paris and completed his studies at the Sorbonne.

While still in Germany, Schneerson had married Haya Mushka, a distant cousin and second daughter of the Lubavitcher rabbi, Joseph Isaac Schneerson. After his marriage, he continued his studies and also worked as secretary to his father-in-law and traveled on his behalf. But World War II caught up to the Schneerson family in France as well.

In 1941, as the Nazis took over Paris, the Schneersons escaped that city and came to New York. Here, Schneerson's father-in-law appointed him head of Lubavitch's educational arm, its social service organization, and its publishing house. It was clear that he was in line to succeed as head rabbi of Habad. When Joseph Isaac died in 1950, however, Menachem Mendel was reluctant, feeling he was not ready. It took him a year to decide to accept the post.

Menachem Mendel Schneerson was the leader of Habad for 44 years. During that time, this small movement, nearly devastated by the Holocaust, grew into a worldwide community of 200,000 members.[38] Schneerson established educational and outreach centers, offered humanitarian aid to all people, and sent emissaries throughout the world to serve the spiritual needs of local Jewish communities. By the beginning of the twenty-first century, there were 1400 Habad/Lubavitch institutions in 35 countries on six continents.

Schneerson's all-inclusive philosophy, combining practical wisdom and spiritual leadership, made him a magnet for many different kinds of people, both Jews and non-Jews. Every Sunday, thousands of visitors lined up to meet him. Some just wanted to be close to the man who, with his piercing eyes, seemed to be able to fathom their secret wishes and needs. Others asked him advice on particular problems.

As the years passed, his fame spread and he advised secular leaders as well as religious followers. The Rebbe, as he was called, turned away no one. In 1983, he began the practice of distributing $1 bills to each person who came to meet him. He explained that he did this to encourage charity, but many kept the dollar bill as a memento, something that had been touched by the great Rebbe himself.

In contrast to the more modern religious thinkers of his age, Schneerson held fast to the idea of a personal Messiah. He believed that this was an age of peace and that it would usher in the Messianic Age. To bring this about even faster, he urged his followers to "do one good deed to hasten Messiah."[39]

Schneerson died in 1994, at the age of 92, revered by his followers and re-spected by all those who came in contact with him. Many in the Habad move-ment believed that Schneerson himself was the Messiah, but as time passed, those convictions faded. After his death, he was granted a Congressional Gold Medal for "outstanding and lasting contributions toward improvements in world education, morality, and acts of charity." The Habad Movement, which he helped build into an empire, is still thriving and growing.

Abraham Joshua Heschel (1907–1972)

Abraham Joshua Heschel was one of the great American Jewish philos-ophers and spiritual leaders. He was from a scholarly Polish family with Hasidic roots but came to Germany to study at the University of Berlin in 1927, where he received a doctorate in the Science of Judaism. In Ger-many, he met Martin Buber who appointed Heschel to succeed him as head of Jewish Adult Education in Frankfurt in 1937. This was not to last long, however, as the Nazis deported Heschel to Poland the next year. Heschel taught in Poland for eight months before immigrating to England, arriv-ing just months before the bombing of Warsaw by the Nazis in September 1939, the official beginning of World War II.

From England, Heschel came to the United States in 1940 and took a post at the Hebrew Union College in Cincinnati, the Rabbinical School of Reform Judaism, where he lectured in Philosophy and Rabbinics. By 1945, he had moved to the Jewish Theological Seminary in New York City, where he taught until his death.

But Abraham Joshua Heschel was more than a teacher. He was a prophet who transcended religious differences and spoke in the name of all human-ity. His passion for social justice brought him into the halls of political power in this country, and he was recognized as a supporter of many just causes.

Heschel believed in equal rights for all and was on the front line when demonstrations were organized in support of the Civil Rights Movement for African Americans in the 1960s. He marched arm in arm with the Rev-erend Martin Luther King, Jr., and used his influence to convince others to join the fight.

When the Vietnam War was an issue in the United States, Heschel joined Clergy and Laity Concerned about Vietnam and urged an end to the war. He insisted that just being against something but doing nothing was not acceptable. "Some are guilty but all are responsible," he said, an allusion to those who were silent during the Holocaust.[40]

The rescue of Soviet Jewry was one of Heschel's causes, too. He worked hard to alert people to the fact that Russia's Jews were in danger. They were the one sizeable remnant of European Jews that had escaped the Nazi slaughter, he pointed out, and now an intolerant communist government threatened their culture and their very existence. Heschel traveled and spoke everywhere on behalf of Russian Jews, urging the U.S. government to use its influence to allow them to emigrate.

In addition to his social activism, Heschel wrote many books. Most of them addressed the spiritual needs of people and the relationship between God and individual human beings. The very titles of his books convey his caring and concern: *Man Is Not Alone, God in Search of Man, Who Is Man?*, and *The Prophets*. He wrote and spoke about the meaning of true religion, and his works appealed to Christians as well as Jews, to non-religious as well as religious people. Religion, he believed, is simply the answer to the ultimate question. "The ultimate meaning of religion," he said, "is to be a religious witness." To be a religious witness entails "compassion for God, reverence for Man, celebration of holiness in time, sensitivity ... to the presence of God in the Bible."

Heschel believed that people today are estranged from religion because they have failed to understand the holy aspect of life, the aspect where the divine meets the human. Through his teachings, Heschel hoped to lead people back to that divine/human reality, and his positive, optimistic approach influenced many. It was said that Heschel "was able to sense glory where others could see only darkness."

Both Christians and Jews recognize Abraham Joshua Heschel, the modern-day prophet, as one of the most influential philosophers of religion in the United States. But most of all, he was a believing Jew who cared about the Jewish people. "Judaism is not a matter of blood or race," he insisted, "but a spiritual dimension of existence, a dimension of holiness. We are messengers, let us not forget our message."

NOTES

1. Dates are always approximate. For the suggested dates of King David's rule, see John Bright, *A History of Israel* (Philadelphia: Westminster Press, 1972), p. 190. Note that *Encyclopaedia Judaica* gives the dates of David's reign as 1010–971 B.C.E.

2. Bright, *A History of Israel*, p. 387.

3. The emphasis was to convince the men to put aside wives because, according to the Torah, men were able to divorce with few restrictions. Women, on the other hand, were not free to divorce their husbands (see Chapter 5).

4. Flavius Josephus, *Jewish War* and *Jewish Antiquities*, in *The Complete Works of Josephus* (Cambridge, Mass.: Harvard University Press, 1925).

5. *Encyclopaedia Judaica* (1st ed.), s.v. "Tannaim."

6. Yigael Yadin, *Bar Kokhba: Rediscovery of the Legendary Hero of the Last Jewish Revolt against Rome* (New York: Random House, 1971).

7. David Goodblatt, "The Beruriah Traditions," *Journal of Jewish Studies* 25 (1975): pp. 68–85.

8. *Encyclopaedia Judaica*, s.v. "Judah haNasi."

9. *Encyclopaedia Judaica*, s.v. "Ashi," and "Amora-im."

10. Judah Goldin, "The Period of the Talmud," in *The Jews, Their History, Culture and Religion*, ed. by Louis Finkelstein (New York: Harper & Bros., 1960), pp. 194–201.

11. Alexander Altmann, "Saadya Gaon," in *Three Jewish Philosophers* (New York: Atheneum, 1969), pp. 113–191 includes excerpts from *The Book of Doctrines and Beliefs.*

12. A full family tree of Rashi's descendants can be found in Esra Shereshevsky, *Rashi: The Man and His World* (New York: Sepher-Hermon Press, 1982), p. 249.

13. Israel Elfenbein, ed., *Teshuvot Rashi* (Hebrew) (New York: Defus Ha-Ahim Shulzinger, 1943), pp. 191–197.

14. Isadore Twersky, *A Maimonides Reader* (New York: Behrman House, 1972), pp. 3–4, 8.

15. Ibid. p. 16. But see *Encyclopaedia Judaica*, s.v. "Maimonides, Moses," who gives the date for completion of the *Mishneh Torah* as 1180.

16. The letter was addressed to Samuel ibn Tibbon, the man who translated *Guide of the Perplexed* into Hebrew. See Twersky, *A Maimonides Reader*, p. 6.

17. *Encyclopaedia Judaica*, *s.v.* "Maimonides, Moses: Biography," citing *Megillat Zuta.*

18. Ibid.

19. Luria's theory of tikkun olam is extremely complicated. For a fuller but brief explanation of the ideas behind Lurianic *Kabbalah*, see Ben Zion Bokser, *The Jewish Mystical Tradition* (New York: Pilgrim Press, 1981), pp. 142–147.

20. *Encyclopaedia Judaica*, s.v. "Shabbetai Zevi: Shabbetai Zevi's Early Years and Personality."

21. Bokser, *The Jewish Mystical Tradition*, p. 178.

22. Emily Taitz, Sondra Henry and Cheryl Tallan, *The JPS Guide to Jewish*

Women: 600 B.C.E.–*1900* C.E. (Philadelphia: Jewish Publication Society, 2003), pp. 134, 136.

23. *Encyclopaedia Judaica,* s.v. "Elijah ben Solomon Zalman: Teachings."

24. This was part of a quote that was placed on a statue of Mendelssohn after his death. See Alexander Altmann, *Moses Mendelssohn: A Biographical Study* (Tuscaloosa: University of Alabama Press, 1973), p. 742.

25. Allan Arkush, *Moses Mendelssohn and the Enlightenment* (Albany: SUNY Press, 1994), p. 221.

26. See Chapter 2, note 4.

27. His most famous work in this style was *Phaedon, oder über die Unsterblichkeit der Seele in drey Gesprächen,* published in 1767.

28. Alfred Jospe, "Moses Mendelssohn" in *Great Jewish Personalities in Modern Times,* ed. Simon Noveck (n.p., B'nai Brith, 1960), p. 27.

29. Jospe, "Moses Mendelssohn," p. 34.

30. Cecil Roth, "Moses Montefiore,'in *Great Jewish Personalities in Modern Times,* ed. Simon Noveck (n.p., B'nai Brith, 1960), p. 46.

31. Lucien Wolf, "Lady Montefiore's Honeymoon," in Lucien Wolf, *Essays in Jewish History,* ed. Cecil Roth (London: Jewish Historical Society of England, 1934), p. 240.

32. Ibid.

33. Marvin Lowenthal, "Theodore Herzl," in *Great Jewish Personalities in Modern Times,* ed. Simon Noveck (n.p., B'nai Brith, 1960), p. 245.

34. Walter Lacqueur, *A History of Zionism* (New York: Schocken Books, 1972), p. 123.

35. *Encyclopaedia Judaica,* s.v. "Kook, Abraham Isaac."

36. Norman Bentwich, "Chaim Weizmann," in *Great Jewish Personalities in Modern Times,* ed. Simon Noveck (n.p., B'nai Brith, 1960), p. 278.

37. *Encyclopaedia Judaica,* s.v. "Buber, Martin."

38. See www.jewishvirtuallibrary.org/jsource/biog/schneerson.

39. Ibid.

40. These and all other quotes from Heschel can be found in Reuven Kimelman, "Abraham Joshua Heschel: Our Generation's Teacher" in *Melton Journal* 15 (Winter, 1983), pp. 3, 23ff.

GLOSSARY

Afikomen: Greek word meaning "dessert." It is traditionally a small piece of matzah (unleavened bread) eaten at the end of the Passover seder.

Aliyah: Hebrew word meaning "ascent." It is used to refer to immigration to the land of Israel and also to the honor of being called up in the synagogue to recite the blessing of the Torah.

Amharic: Language of the Ethiopian Jews.

Amidah: Prayer included in the daily and holiday services. It is recited silently, standing up. (The word Amidah means "standing.")

Amora-im: Scholars who compiled the Gemara, commentary on the Mishnah.

Aramaic: Ancient, northwestern Semitic language. It was the principal language of the land of Israel from approximately 300 B.C.E. to the early centuries of the Common Era and is the language of the Talmud.

Ashkenazim: Jews who lived in Germany or Eastern Europe and whose common language was Yiddish.

Baal Shem Tov: Master of the Divine Name. This title was given to Israel ben Eliezer, the founder of Hasidism.

Balfour Declaration: Decree issued by England on November 2, 1917, when Lord Arthur James Balfour was foreign secretary. It read, in part, that "His majesty's government view with favor the establishment in Palestine of a national home for the Jewish people and will use their best endeavors to facilitate the achievement of that object."

Bar/Bat Mitzvah: Coming-of-age ceremony for Jewish boys and girls at the age of 13.

Bet Din: Jewish court, consisting of three rabbis and convened to adjudicate issues concerning Jewish law.

Birkat haMazon: Blessing recited by Jews after a meal.

Brit/Bris: Act of circumcising a baby boy and the ceremony surrounding it. It is performed when the baby is eight days old as a sign and a remembrance of Abraham's original covenant with God.

Brit haBat: Ceremony of recent tradition, meant to be the parallel of the brit for boy babies, welcoming baby girls into the covenant.

Canaan: Name by which the land of Israel was originally known before God's promise to Abraham and the return of the Israelites from Egypt.

Damascus Affair: Events surrounding the accusation, in 1840, that Syrian Jews had kidnapped a Catholic friar and murdered him to use his blood in Jewish ritual. A Jew was arrested and tortured until he gave the names of several others. The incident shocked Jews throughout the world, as well as western Christians, and prompted a visit by the unofficial Jewish troubleshooter, Moses Montefiore of England, at the head of a delegation. He appealed to the leaders of Egypt and arranged for the release of those Jews who were still alive.

Davidic Line: Family line that traced their ancestry back to King David. They were considered the only legitimate rulers when the Messiah came and a new dynasty would be established in the land of Israel.

Essenes: Ascetic group of Jews who lived in the land of Israel at the beginning of the Common Era.

Gan Eden: Garden of Eden. One of the names used for the World to Come, or life after death.

Gaon (Gaonim): Title given to the heads of the academies in Babylonia, bestowed only on the greatest scholars of the community.

Gemara: Commentary and explanation of the Mishnah. The Mishnah and Gemara together make up the Talmud.

Get: Divorce.

Giehinnom: Hebrew word that is the rough equivalent of hell. It is considered a temporary place where the wicked go until the Messiah comes and ushers in the Golden Age.

Gloss: Series of comments and explanations added to a text.

Habad: Alternative name for the Lubavitcher Hasidim. It is an acronym whose letters stand for the Hebrew words hesed (lovingkindness), binah (understanding), and da-at (knowledge).

Haftarah: Addition to the regular Torah reading, recited on Sabbaths and holidays after the reading of the designated portion of the Torah. It is usually a passage from the books of the Prophets.

Hagaddah: Book telling the story of Passover and describing the associated rituals for the seder.

Hai: "Life"; in Hebrew, also, the number eighteen.

Hasidim: Jewish sect that originated in southern Poland in the eighteenth century and spread throughout Eastern Europe.

Hasmoneans: Dynasty of the Maccabees and their descendants. They ruled an independent Jewish state from 165 B.C.E. until the Romans officially took over the area in 63 B.C.E.

Havdalah: Ceremony ushering out the Sabbath on Saturday evening.

Hevra Kadisha: Group of Jews in a Jewish community that takes responsibility for washing and preparing the bodies of the dead before burial.

Huppah: Canopy under which a Jewish wedding ceremony is performed.

Kabbalah: System of mystical beliefs and practices to bring Jews closer to God. It is also used to refer to the body of literature discussing these systems and beliefs and describing various magical methods.

Kaddish: Prayer for the dead recited at the funeral and subsequently during the period of mourning.

Kashrut (Kosher): Laws of food purity, including restrictions on eating certain kinds of meat and separating meat from milk.

Ketubbah: Jewish marriage contract ensuring the rights of the wife in marriage. In the past, the ketubbah also stipulated the dowry the bride brought to the marriage and the amount of money promised by the groom. In modern times, this document is more ceremonial but is still a requirement of a Jewish marriage.

Kiddush: Extended blessing over wine, recited on Sabbaths and holidays.

Kippah: Small skullcap worn by observant Jews, especially in synagogue, or whenever praying or studying. In Yiddish it is called a *yarmulka*.

Kohen (Kohanim): Hereditary group of Jewish men who were given the honor of officiating at the rites in the Holy Temple. They were part of the tribe of Levi and were the direct descendants of Aaron, Moses's brother.

Kol Nidre: Prayer recited on the eve of Yom Kippur, asking God to forgive all unfulfilled vows.

Lulav: Palm frond, tied together with three other species of plants from the land of Israel, used on the holiday of Sukkot as a symbol of fertility.

Maariv: Daily evening service, held at sundown.

Maccabees: Mattathias and his five sons, Simon, Eliezer, Judah, John, and Jonathan, heroes of the Hanukkah story.

Menorah: Originally a seven-branched candelabrum used in the Holy Temple. It was one of the earliest symbols of the Jews. In modern times, a menorah usually refers to a candelabrum with nine places for candles, used exclusively for the celebration of Hanukkah. It is also called a Hanukkiah.

Mezuzot: Plural of mezuzah, a small holder affixed to the doorpost of a Jewish home and containing the full text of the passage from Deuteronomy 6:6–9 and the Sh'ma prayer.

Minhah: Late afternoon daily service, usually held just before sundown and joined with the Maariv (evening) service.

Minyan: Quorum of ten needed for full prayer service. Traditionally, the requirement was for ten men, but since the 1970s some synagogues count women as part of a minyan.

Mishloah Manot: Giving of gifts, usually pastries and other food, on the holiday of Purim.

Mishnah: Set of six volumes explaining and commenting on biblical law. Often referred to as the oral law because, before it was written down, it was an oral tradition passed down from one generation to another.

Mitnagdim: Literally, "the opposers." In the late eighteenth century, it referred to those Jews who took a position against the early Hasidim.

Mitzvah/Mitzvot: Although often translated as "good deeds," this word means "commandment(s)". *Mitzvot* can be positive, things one is required to do, or negative, things one must not do. Sages have counted a total of 613 *mitzvot* enumerated in the Bible. They are discussed in the Talmud and in numerous other Jewish law codes.

Mohel: Expert who performs ritual circumcisions.

Musaf: Additional part of the service immediately after the Torah service on Sabbaths and festivals.

Ne'ilah: Final service of Yom Kippur, ending just at sunset.

Olam haBa: World to Come. This refers to life after death, or after the coming of the Messiah and the Golden Age.

Pikuah Nefesh: Safeguarding a soul, implying the saving of a life. This principle overrides every Jewish law. For example, it enables a doctor to break the Sabbath laws to care for a patient; it allows individuals to help in an accident at any time, or to eat even ritually unclean food if they are faced with starvation.

Pogrom: Organized attack on Jews.

Polygyny: Practice of taking more than one wife at a time. Polygyny is different from polygamy, as polygamy implies that either spouse may take multiple partners. This was never the case in Judaism, which allowed this option only for men.

Rambam: Alternative name for Rabbi Moses ben Maimon (Maimonides), one of the most respected sages and authors in Judaism. Following popular usage, this name is taken from the acronym (the first initials) Rabbi Moshe ben Maimon.

Rashi: Acronym for the great medieval Jewish sage, Rabbi Shlomo Yitzhaki. Rashi is the name by which he is most commonly known.

Rebbe: Yiddish form of the Hebrew "Rav" (meaning master or scholar), and used to refer to the charismatic leaders of the Hasidim.

Romaniot: Jews who lived in Greece, Turkey, and the Balkans. They are often confused with the Sephardim because, after the expulsion from Spain, many Sephardim moved to that area and culturally overpowered the original Jewish inhabitants.

Rosh Hodesh: Literally, "the head of the month," the beginning of each month of the Jewish lunar calendar, marked by the appearance of the new moon. Jews have often considered it as a half-holiday, especially for women. Tradition says it was a reward for the women who, in biblical times, donated their gold jewelry to build the Ark of the Covenant.

Sadducees: Division of Jews dating from the first century before the Common Era. They generally represented the upper classes and were opposed by the larger but less powerful branch, the Pharisees, who represented the common people.

Sandek: Sponsor of infant being circumcised. The sandek's main role in the brit ceremony is to hold the baby while the mohel performs the circumcision.

Savora-im: Babylonian sages who completed the editing of the Talmud in the fifth century of the Common Era. They are credited with determining the final arrangement, organizing it according to the six major orders of the Mishnah, and then dividing it into 63 separate books

Seder: Ceremonial meal on the first and second nights of Passover.

Sephardim: Jews who lived in Spain and Portugal before the expulsions of 1492 and 1497.

Shabbat: Sabbath.

Sh'ma: One-line prayer recited by Jews each morning, twice during each day, and at other times, proclaiming the unity of God. The text is: "Hear O Israel, the Lord our God is One."

Shaharit: Morning service.

Shehehiyanu prayer: Prayer praising God for a special event or achievement. The prayer thanks God "who has kept us alive and brought us to this time." She-hehiyanu, one of the words in this prayer, means, literally, "who has kept us alive."

Shofar: Instrument traditionally made from the horn of a ram. In early Israelite history, it was blown as an alarm to alert the people. In modern times, it is blown during daily morning services in the month of Elul (the month preceding the High Holidays), several times at the service on Rosh HaShanah, and once at the end of the Yom Kippur service.

Siddur: Jewish prayer book, containing the order of prayers for weekdays, Sabbaths, and holidays. There are many versions of the siddur. Each branch uses its own version. In addition, most prayer books include a side-by-side translation into the language spoken in their own community. Some also have transliterations, a transference of the Hebrew words into the local alphabet, for those who cannot read Hebrew.

Sitting Shivah: Observance of the seven days of mourning immediately after the death of a close relative. It is the custom for people to visit the mourners during this week.

Sukkah: Special hut built for the holiday of Sukkot, intended as a reminder of the Exodus from Egypt. It must have a roof open to the stars and is usually covered only with branches or reeds. Often it is decorated with fruits, vegetables, and flowers as a sign of the harvest that occurs in the land of Israel at this time.

Tallit: Prayer shawl worn by Jews during prayer, with fringes on the four corners according to the rule laid out in the Bible. The fringes are meant to be a reminder of the laws of God.

Tallit Katan: Small tallit with fringes, worn under the shirt by Orthodox Jewish men.

Talmud: Compilation of Jewish law composed of the Mishnah and the Gemara.

Tanakh: Acronym for the complete Hebrew Bible, made up of Torah (the Five Books of Moses), Nevi'im (Prophets), and Ketuvim (Writings).

Tanna-im: Sages whose discussions and decisions make up the laws and stories of the Mishnah. They were followed by the Amora-im, interpreters of the Mishnah.

Tefillin: Phylacteries—two small boxes containing the words of the Sh'ma prayer. The boxes are attached to leather straps and wrapped around the head and the left arm. Tefillin are primarily used by Orthodox men during morning prayer, from the time of bar mitzvah.

Torah: First five books of the Bible, sometimes called "The Five Books of Moses." Over the centuries, the word Torah has become a synonym for all of Jewish learning, so the study of Torah often implies the study of all Jewish law.

Tzaddik: Righteous person. Tzaddik was used as an honorific for the leaders of the individual Hasidic communities during the late 1700s and 1800s. An alternate title was "rebbe."

Tzedakah: Hebrew word for "righteousness." It also has the meaning of "charity," so the expression "give to tzedakah" means to give money to charity.

Yarmulka: See *kippah*.

Zion: Name of one of the mountains in the city of Jerusalem. It is also another word for Jerusalem itself. Later, it came to symbolize all of the land of Israel, with Jerusalem as its capital.

Zionism: Philosophy that Jews belong in their own land and the political effort to achieve that goal.

The Zohar: The Book of Splendor is the principal text of Kabbalah. Its author is believed to have been the Spanish kabbalist Moses ben Shem Tov de Leon, who lived during the late thirteenth century, but this has never been definitively confirmed.

BIBLIOGRAPHY

Altmann, Alexander. *Moses Mendelssohn: A Biographical Study.* Tuscaloosa, Ala.: University of Alabama Press, 1973.

Altmann, Alexander, ed. "Saadya Gaon." In *Three Jewish Philosophers.* New York: Atheneum, 1969.

The American Jewish Year Book, vols. 102 and 103. Binghamton, N.Y.: American Jewish Committee, 2002 and 2003.

Ankori, Zvi. *Karaites in Byzantium: The Formative Years, 970–1100.* New York: AMS Press, 1968.

Arkush, Allan. *Moses Mendelssohn and the Englightenment.* Albany, N.Y.: SUNY Press, 1994.

Bein, Alex. *The Return to the Soil: A History of Jewish Settlement in Israel.* Jerusalem: Youth and Hechalutz Dept of the Zionist Organization, 1952.

Ben Sasson, H.H., ed. *A History of the Jewish People.* Cambridge, Mass.: Harvard University Press, 1976.

Berger, Elmer. *Judaism or Jewish Nationalism: The Alternative to Zionism.* New York: Bookman Association, 1957.

Bokser, Ben Zion. *The Jewish Mystical Tradition.* New York: Pilgrim Press, 1981.

Bonfils, Robert. *Jewish Life in Renaissance Italy.* Berkeley: University of California Press, 1994.

Bowman, Steven. *The Jews of Byzantium: 1204–1354.* Tuscaloosa, Ala.: University of Alabama Press, 1985.

Bright, John. *A History of Israel*, 2nd ed. Philadelphia: Westminster Press, 1972.

Buber, Martin. *I and Thou*. Edinburgh: T & T Clark, 1937.

Buber, Martin. *Tales of the Hasidim*. New York: Schocken Books, 1958; 1991.

Carmi, T. *The Penguin Book of Hebrew Verse*. New York: Penguin Press, 1981.

Chazan, Robert, and Marc Lee Raphael, eds. *Modern Jewish History: A Source Reader*. New York: Schocken Books, 1974.

Cohen, Debra Nussbaum. "Renewal's Struggle for Acceptance," *The Jewish Week*, 21 April, 2000, 1.

Davidowicz, Lucy S. *The Golden Tradition: Jewish Life and Thought in Eastern Europe*. Boston: Beacon Press, 1967.

Diamant, Anita. *The New Jewish Wedding*. New York: Summit Books, 1985.

Eban, Aba. *My People: The Story of the Jews*. New York: Behrman House and Random House, 1968.

Eisenstein, Ira. *Reconstructing Judaism: An Autobiography*. New York: Reconstructionist Press, 1986.

Elbogen, Ismar. *Jewish Liturgy: A Comprehensive History*. Translated by Raymond P. Scheindlein. Philadelphia: Jewish Publication Society, 1993.

Elfenbein, Israel, ed. *Teshuvot Rashi* (Hebrew). New York: Defus Ha-Ahim Shulzinger, 1943.

Encyclopaedia Judaica, 16 volumes. Jerusalem and New York: Keter and Macmillan, 1971–72.

Finkelstein, Israel, and Neil Asher Silberman. *The Bible Unearthed: Archeology's New Vision of Ancient Israel and the Origin of Its Sacred Texts*. Atlanta: Free Press, 2001.

Finkelstein, Louis. *Jewish Self-Government in the Middle Ages*. New York: Philipp Feldheim, 1964.

Freund, Michael. "How Wen-Jing Became 'Shalva': Chinese Jewish Descendant Returns to Judaism." *Jerusalem Post*, 22 June, 2004, 5.

Friedman, Mordecai A. *Jewish Marriage in Palestine: A Cairo Geniza Study*. 2 vols. Tel Aviv: Tel Aviv University Press, 1980.

Gaster, Theodore H. *Festivals of the Jewish Year*. New York: William Sloane Assoc., 1952; 4th printing, 1968.

Goldin, Judah. "The Period of the Talmud." In *The Jews, Their History, Culture and Religion*, ed. Louis Finkelstein. New York: Harper & Bros., 1960.

Goodman, Philip and Hanna. *The Jewish Marriage Anthology*. Philadelphia: Jewish Publication Society, 1965.

Grayzel, Solomon. *A History of the Jews from the Babylonian Exile to the Present*. Philadelphia: The Jewish Publication Society, 1947; reprint 1968.

Grayzel, Solomon. *The Church and the Jews in the XIIIth Century,* Vol. 2. Detroit: Wayne State University Press, 1989.

Grunfeld, I. ed. and trans. *Three Generations: The Influence of Samson Rafael Hirsch on Jewish Life and Thought.* London: Jewish Post Publications, 1958.

Harran, Don. "Jewish Musical Culture: Leon de Modena." In *The Jews of Early Modern Venice,* ed. Robert C. Davis and Benjamin Ravid. Baltimore: Johns Hopkins University Press, 2001.

Hauptman, Judith. *Rereading the Rabbis: Woman's Voice.* Boulder, Col.: Westview Press, 1998.

Isaacs, Ronald H. *Rites of Passage: A Guide to the Jewish Life Cycle.* Hoboken, N.J.: K'tav, 1992.

Josephus, Flavius. *The Complete Works of Josephus: Jewish War* and *Jewish Antiquities.* Cambridge, Mass.: Harvard University Press, 1925.

Kaplan, Mordecai. *Judaism as a Civilization.* Philadelphia: Jewish Publication Society, 1934; new ed. 1994.

Kaplan, Mordecai. *The Meaning of God in Modern Jewish Religion.* 1937; new ed. Detroit: Wayne State University Press, 1994.

Kaplan, Mordecai. *The Purpose and Meaning of Jewish Existence.* Philadelphia: Jewish Publication Society, 1964.

Kimelman, Reuven. "Abraham Joshua Heschel: Our Generation's Teacher." *Melton Journal* 15 (1983): 3, 23f; also available at www.crosscurrents. org/heschel.htm.

Krohn, Paysach J. *Bris Milah.* New York: Mesorah Publications, 1984.

Lacqueur, Walter. *A History of Zionism.* New York: Schocken Books, 1972.

Lamm, Maurice. *The Jewish Way in Death and Mourning.* New York: Jonathan David Publishers, 1969.

Lerner, Michael. *Jewish Renewal: A Path to Healing and Transformation.* New York: G. P. Putnam's Sons, 1994.

Neusner, Jacob. *There We Sat Down: Talmudic Judaism in the Making.* New York: K'tav, 1972.

Noveck, Simon, ed. *Great Jewish Personalities in Modern Times.* n.p., B'nai Brith, 1960.

Plaut, W. Gunther. *The Growth of Reform Judaism.* New York: World Union for Progressive Judaism, 1965.

Plaut, W. Gunther. *The Rise of Reform Judaism.* New York: World Union for Progressive Judaism, 1963.

Primak, Karen, ed. *Under One Canopy: Readings in Jewish Diversity.* New York: Kulanu, 2003.

Scholem, Gershom. *Major Trends in Jewish Mysticism*, 3rd ed. New York: Schocken Books, 1954.

Segal, Ariel. *Jews of the Amazon: Self Exile in Paradise.* Philadelphia: Jewish Publication Society, 1999.

Shereshevsky, Ezra. *Rashi: The Man and his World.* New York: Sepher-Hermon Press, 1982.

Siddur Sim Shalom, ed. and trans. Jules Harlow. New York: United Synagogue of America, 1985.

Stillman, Norman A. *The Jews of Arab Lands: A History and Source Book.* Philadelphia: Jewish Publication Society, 1979.

Stow, Kenneth. *Alienated Minority: The Jews of Medieval Latin Europe.* Cambridge, Mass.: Harvard University Press, 1992.

Swidler, Leonard. *Women in Judaism: The Status of Women in Formative Judaism.* Metuchen, N.J.: Scarecrow Press, 1976.

Taitz, Emily, Sondra Henry, and Cheryl Tallan. *The JPS Guide to Jewish Women: 600 B.C.E.–1900 C.E.* Philadelphia: Jewish Publication Society, 2003.

Taitz, Emily, and Sondra Henry. *Remarkable Jewish Women: Rebels, Rabbis and Other Women from Biblical Times to the Present*, 2nd ed. New York: Biblio Press, 2001.

Tcherikover, Victor. *Hellenistic Civilisation and the Jews*, trans. S. Applebaum. New York: Atheneum, 1977.

The Torah: The Five Books of Moses. Philadelphia: Jewish Publication Society, 1977.

Twersky, Isadore. *A Maimonides Reader.* New York: Behrman House, 1972.

Wagaw, Teshome G. *For Our Soul: Ethiopian Jews in Israel.* Detroit: Wayne State University Press, 1993.

Waxman, Mordecai, ed. *Tradition and Change: The Development of Conservative Judaism.* New York: Burning Bush Press, 1958.

Weinryb, Bernard D. *The Jews of Poland: A Social and Economic History of the Jewish Community in Poland from 1100–1800.* Philadelphia: Jewish Publication Society, 1982.

Wellhausen, Julius. *Prolegomena to the History of Israel.* New York: Meridian Books, 1957.

Wiesel, Elie. *The Jews of Silence*, trans. Neal Kozodoy. New York: Signet Books, 1967.

Wolpe, David J. *Why Be Jewish?* New York: Henry Holt and Co., 1995.

Xin, Xu with Beverly Friend. *Legends of the Chinese Jews of Kaifeng.* Hoboken, N.J.: K'tav, 1995.

Yadin, Yigael. *Bar Kokhba: Rediscovery of the Legendary Hero of the Last Jewish Revolt against Rome.* New York: Random House, 1971.

WEB SITES

Jewish Virtual Library (A Division of the American-Israeli Cooperative Enterprise), http://www.jewishvirtuallibrary.org/source/Judaism/uganda1.html, or http://www.jewishvirtuallibrary.org/jsource/biog/schneerson.

National Havurah Committee, http://www.havurah.org.

The Scribe: The Magazine of Babylonian Jewry, http://www.dangoor.com/72page25.html.

INDEX

About the Authors

EMILY TAITZ is an independent scholar and author of *The Jews of Medieval France: The Community of Champagne* (Greenwood, 1994) and numerous essays on Judaism and the coauthor of *Remarkable Jewish Women: Rebels, Rabbis and Other Women from Biblical Times to the Present* (2002), among other works.

RANDALL L. NADEAU is Associate Professor of East Asian Religions at Trinity University, San Antonio, Texas.

JOHN M. THOMPSON teaches in the Department of Philosophy and Religious Studies, Christopher Newport University, Newport News, Virginia.

LEE W. BAILEY is Associate Professor of Philosophy and Religion at Ithaca College.

ZAYN R. KASSAM is Associate Professor of Religious Studies and Chair of the Religious Studies Department, Pomona College.

STEVEN J. ROSEN is an independent scholar and prolific writer on Hinduism.